# *Chocolate*
## *for* **LENT**

# *Chocolate*
# *for* LENT

*By*
*Hilary Brand*

BOOKS & MEDIA
Boston

**Library of Congress Cataloging-in-Publication Data**

Brand, Hilary.
  Chocolate for Lent / by Hilary Brand.
      p. cm.
Rev. ed. of: Christ and the chocolaterie. Includes bibliographical references (p. 137).
  ISBN 0-8198-1567-5
  1. Lent—Prayer-books and devotions—English. 2. Chocolat (Motion picture) I. Brand, Hilary. Christ and the chocolaterie. II. Title.
  BX2170.L4B73 2004
  242'.34—dc22

                                                    2003014083

Cover design: Regina Frances Dick, FSP
Cover photo: Mary Emmanuel Alves, FSP

"P" and Pauline are registered trademarks of the Daughters of St. Paul.

Published by Darton, Longman and Todd, London, UK, 2002

Published in the U.S.A. by Pauline Books & Media, 50 Saint Paul's Avenue, Boston, MA 02130-3491. Printed in the U.S.A.

www.pauline.org

Pauline Books & Media is the publishing house of the Daughters of St. Paul, an international congregation of women religious serving the Church with the communications media.

3  4  5  6  7  8  9                    12  11 10  09  08 07

# Contents

# Introduction

### The Power of a Story

Some people think that fiction has nothing to teach us. "It isn't true," they say. What they mean is that it is not factual. But just because something is not factual does not mean it doesn't have truths to teach us. In fact, very often it is just the reverse.

Suppose you were asked to write a history of your parish church. You would not find it difficult to write the facts: number in the congregation, the different activities, names of leaders, etc. You probably wouldn't find it too difficult to write the good things: we've had an adult faith formation course, we've built a new church hall, we take our CYO kids camping. But quite probably, and quite rightly, you would find it hard to be totally honest. What about the difficult things—the tensions between the pastor and the organist, the time the parish council leader got offended and walked out, the youth leader who left his wife for a fling with a CCD teacher?

If you were writing fiction, however, you could explore these difficult things. You could examine how the youth leader ached for some human warmth, what there was in the parish council leader's childhood that made her so touchy, how the pastor went home at night and wept with frustration at trying to keep everyone happy. It might be a far truer account of how things really are in your parish than an accurate but safe history that doesn't offend anyone.

"But come on," some others will say, when confronted with a film like *Chocolat*, "This is Hollywood! This is nothing like real life!" True, in some ways it isn't. Rootless travelers seldom return to settle down (and are rarely quite as charming as Juliette Binoche and Johnny Depp), kleptomaniacs are rarely cured as quickly as Josephine Muscat, people hardly make friends with their enemies as quickly as the Comte does with Vianne. We must allow the silver screen its exaggerations and neatly knotted loose ends—we are, after all, encroaching on the world of myths and legends. But then, myths and legends have a great deal to teach us.

It was Aristotle who first defined the value of myth's role. He described it as "catharsis," a word that means literally a purification or purging. What Aristotle meant was that by identifying with the drama, the audience is provided with a safe place to draw out and examine buried feeling—anger, fear, pain, lust—which, exploding in another context, could be dangerous. A screenwriter acquaintance of mine describes his work as follows: "I want to make people feel so much that they start to think."

Many films are great starting points for exploring profound issues about God, the world, and what it means to be human. If this lenten program does nothing more than introduce a few more people to the depths that even a fairly light and frivolous movie can plumb, then it will have done its job.

## The Strength of an Image

Movies, like the Bible, are crammed full of visual metaphors. Often, as in the Bible, they use elemental images—sun, rain, fire, wind, grain, wine—to "speak" of some abstract concept—blessing, testing, passion, change, strength, joy—in a deeper way than words ever could. Occasionally a movie thrusts these images at you so that you cannot miss them. But often it does not; mostly, they are fleeting and seemingly accidental. In reality, they are never accidental. When it costs tens of thousands of dollars for even a few moments of movie footage, you can be certain that absolutely everything you see and hear is completely intentional. You may not consciously "read" these images at all, and the director knows you will not, but subconsciously, they will do their work.

So as you view *Chocolat* (and to fully benefit from this lenten program, you will need to see the entire movie before beginning), you may find it interesting and instructive to watch for these sorts of images and sounds

xii CHOCOLATE FOR LENT

as the movie progresses. Why are they there? What are they saying?

## The Depth of a Character

At a screenwriting class I attended, I was told that when I created my characters, I needed to "know them as well as God knows them." Good screenwriters will work out a complete biography of each of the film's major characters: what their childhood was like, what their formative experiences were, what it is deep down that drives them. They would know, for example, what it was like for the Comte in *Chocolat* to grow up learning of his illustrious forebears, knowing he had to follow their example. They would know how Anouk felt in the school playgrounds of Vienna and Andalusia. Sometimes this information never even appears in the film, but often it does.

Often there are little clues to tell where this person is coming from and what it is that makes them behave the way they do. Watch for these kinds of clues as you view *Chocolat*. They will throw light on the characters' actions and, by doing so, may even throw light on your own!

## The Benefit of Repeated Viewing

You will see even from the examples I have given above that there is far more in any movie than you are likely to absorb in one sitting. This program allows for one full viewing of the movie, plus excerpts during each session. However, if you can find time to view the movie by yourself a second or even third time, you will probably find it rewarding. For group leaders, a second full viewing is almost essential.

In case your memory needs jogging, here is a list of the movie's main characters:

| | |
|---|---|
| Vianne | the journeying chocolate maker; daughter of Chitza and George |
| Anouk | her daughter |
| Comte de Reynaud | the Mayor of Lasquenet |
| Roux | the 'river rat' |
| Armande Voizin | old lady with diabetes, Caroline's mother |
| Caroline Clairmont | daughter of Armande, mother to Luc, secretary to the Comte |
| Serge Muscat | drunken cafe owner |
| Josephine Muscat | Serge's battered wife |
| Guillaume Blerot | retired gentleman with dog, Charlie |
| Madame Audel | widow to whom Guillaume is attracted |
| Père Henri | priest |
| Yvette Marceau | wife starving for physical affection |
| Alphonse Marceau | weary husband |

## A Safe Environment

When I mentioned the value of film earlier, I spoke of "catharsis" and the value of an appropriate environment in which to allow deep issues to surface. In taking *Chocolat* out of the darkened cinema or the privacy of your living room and examining it together in depth, are we therefore creating an unsafe environment?

I have been to many church meetings that were heavy on the "cringe factor". Do you know the kind? The "turn to the person next to you and tell them how God has blessed you" syndrome. I have cringed frequently enough not to wish to impose it on you here.

I know that you may not wish to bare your soul to a stranger, and even less to an acquaintance whom you greet occasionally at the church door or at the post office. But I also know that, at their best, parishes are real communities where people can relate to each other on an honest and accepting level. After all, if we can't do it here, where we are assured that God loves us, complete with all our baggage and failings, then where can we do it?

I have tried, therefore, to create an atmosphere that gives you the freedom to speak honestly, yet without compelling you to do so if you are not comfortable. But try to have courage, because often when you share something difficult, you will find it will immediately echo in the hearts of those listening.

However, hearing someone else's honest sharing brings with it responsibilities:

» First, *confidentiality*. It cannot be a safe environment if the speaker fears that what he or she says will be repeated and dissected elsewhere.

» Second, *respect*. Even though you feel you may have great wisdom on a subject, never pounce on someone with advice and pat answers. Resist the urge to tell anyone in the group that they are wrong. Respectful questions, perhaps, but never condemnatory statements. (Incidentally, see how Vianne tackles this kind of situation in the film.)

» Third, *genuine listening* is often the greatest gift you can offer someone. Give each speaker your whole attention. Resist the urge to think about what you want to say next. Let other people's words sink in rather than float over you and you will be enriched by the experience of sharing.

## The Meaning of Community

The word "community" is often used to describe a group of people who just happen to be thrown together by geography or by a common interest. *True* community, however, is far deeper—and quite rare. The following definition, based on the writings of M. Scott Peck, seems to me to encapsulate what the film *Chocolat* and this program is about: "We define community as a group of people who, regardless of their backgrounds and beliefs, have been able to accept and transcend their differences, enabling them to communicate effectively and openly."

Such acceptance and transcendence can usually only happen when differences are aired in the first place—a risky business. But it is God who can provide the courage to take such a risk and God who is in the midst when true community happens. I hope that as your group embarks on this lenten journey, it will enable you, too, to become community for each other and that you will discover it to be a life-giving experience.

### The Blessings and Barbs of The Book

The book I am referring to is not the book *Chocolat*, on which the movie is based (see below), but the Bible. You will find that each week's section includes a suggested reading that introduces the topic, and one to follow your reflection afterwards. And each of these includes a scripture passage (almost always about the things that Jesus did or said).

Now, I know from experience, not least my own, that the one thing most people quickly skip over is the scripture passages. Yes, I can imagine how busy you are, and I expect many of you may be familiar with the passages.

But probably not as familiar as you think! The reason the words and actions of Jesus have so much power is because they have many layers. Their simplicity is deceptive. What spoke to you in a certain way the last time you read or heard it may have more to say today. So, I implore you, try to do more than skim over the gospel passages. At least now and then, give yourself a bit of time and space to mull them over.

They may contain some hard sayings. They may raise more questions than answers. But I'd be prepared to bet on it: read the Scriptures reflectively, and nine times out of ten, you will be surprised by the result.

## P.S.: Book versus Movie

Many people may have read the original book *Chocolat*, by Joanne Harris. I'm sorry to disappoint you if the book is a favorite, but this program completely ignores it. This is not because it is not a good book, but rather because book and film are quite different. The book is set in the present day and the film in the late 1950s. Some characters in the book are compacted into one in the film, or are changed in some way. Also, the endings are different. So to avoid confusion, this program focuses entirely on the film.

## How to Use This Program

Each week of the program is divided into three parts. The first, "To Start Your Reflection" is for individual reading before the group meets. Then comes the session outline, followed by "To Continue Your Reflection" to be read individually afterwards. When it comes to the group session, everyone can follow the outline in his or her copy of the book, with the leader reading aloud the questions and their introductions.

You will see that the book contains two main sections: the first is for all participants and the second is just for group leaders. If you are a group leader, you may need to flip back and forth between the two during the meeting (although hopefully you will have read the leader's notes thoroughly beforehand). If you are not the leader, then resist the urge to look at the notes—you will get more out of the group if you think for yourself rather than look for the answers. Not that the leader's notes provide all the answers anyway; I have only offered prompts or hints where I felt they were really necessary. The point of this program is to provoke thought and discussion, not to arrive at "correct" conclusions.

## Week One

# Giving Up—
# The Prelude to Change

## To Start Your Reflection

I love chocolate. Dark and bitter, rich and creamy, lemon creams, mint thins, caramels, truffles, pralines, profiteroles, Mars bars, Mississippi mud pies…even the names make my mouth water. Caramels, fudge, dream bars and M&M's…I'll take *all* of them *all* the time.

I also weigh 180 pounds.

I am appalled to see this statement in print, but I gathered up my courage and put it here for a good reason. I want to make an honest admission that, where food is concerned, I am very bad indeed at giving up. Or, put another way, where diets and exercise are concerned, I am very good at giving up!

I am telling you this to explain that, wonderful as chocolate is, for me it can quite genuinely become an addiction. I know that food is the first thing I turn to when I am stressed, and that the wrong sort of food makes me sluggish and slobbish, a Jabba the Hutt look-alike.

I am all too aware that because there is more of me than there ought to be, in other aspects there is perhaps less of me than there could be. I know that when I eat less and exercise more, I have more energy to put into my life. I know that unless I shed a few pounds, I will never be able to see the sunrise from the top of Mount Sinai, wear the latest fashions, or dance without feeling silly—all things I would love to do.

I begin this way to show you one reason at least why *Chocolat's* seductive celebration of "if it feels good, do it" needs to be seen with a somewhat critical eye. (Another reason, of course, is the fact that much of the chocolate we eat in the West is produced in the Third World in conditions of near slavery. (See p. 123, "The Unfair Economics of Chocolate.")

The film's philosophy of indulging yourself, enjoying life, and learning to be yourself very much taps into the "spirit of our age." Now, there are some very healthy aspects to all of those things. All the same, my knowledge of the Christian faith leads me to wonder whether we should jettison self-denial that easily. It is all too easy to accept the "feel good" message of a movie without thinking. Perhaps we should first explore whether the idea of "giving something up for Lent"—be it chocolate, wine, television, or sex—is valid. Is it even Christian?

## Origins of Lent

The name 'Lent' comes from the Saxon word *Lencten-tid,* used for the month of March and signifying spring-time and the lengthening of days. The idea of a fast before Easter, however, goes way back before Christianity reached the Saxons, to the first centuries of the Church. It seems to have sprung up spontaneously, albeit only practiced for two or three days before Easter at first.

The earliest known reference to a forty-day fast was in 325 A.D. as one of the 'canons' (church rules) arising from the Council of Nicaea, where church leaders from all of the then-Christian world met to thrash out a mutual understanding of what they believed. It became common practice that for forty days only one meal a day was eaten, with no meat or fish. (As to whether chocolate was allowed, see p. 117, "The Curious History of Chocolate"!)

The forty days, of course, is an echo of Christ's time of fasting in the wilderness. But Christ never commanded his followers to fast, and neither did the apostles. (Jesus did recognize it as a common practice, however, saying "*when* you fast," rather than "*if* you fast" in Matthew 6:16).

So why did the practice arise? The main reason seems to be that early Church, baptisms only happened once a year, at Easter. Lent was instituted as a preparation for Baptism—the public initiation into the Christian faith—and for those who wanted to renew their baptismal commitment.

Christ's fast in the wilderness had a purpose. It was a preparation for a major change in his life: the beginning of a ministry that would change the face of history. When Christ called his followers to give anything up, that too was in order to set them free to follow a new direction. "Giving up" was so that they might be radically changed—and that their change would then change their world. In the first centuries of Christendom, Lent was a time of "giving up" as preparation for a major life change.

## Personal Reflection

*Note: This is an exercise in imagination; there are no right or wrong answers. These questions will be discussed during the group encounter.*

*Read Matthew 4:1–11, 18–22.*

- What would have happened if Jesus had *not* withdrawn to the desert and been tempted for forty days before he began his ministry?

- What would have happened if Peter and Andrew, James and John had *not* given up the security of their employment and followed Jesus?

As well as pondering the above, if you have time, read the following scripture passage and reflect on the following question. Both will be discussed during the group session.

***Read Mark 10:17–27.***

➤ What might have happened if the rich young man had given away everything that he owned and embarked on a new life?

➤ What may have happened to him if he did not?

# Group Encounter

*View movie clip*                                    (5 min.)

**Scenes:** Chocolate beans awakening a weary husband's passion for his toilet-scrubbing wife; Comte in his study, refusing food; Josephine going into the chocolaterie; Guillaume meeting three widows.

*Discuss*                                        (20–30 min.)

1.  What motivates the Comte's frugal diet? Is it his own physical, mental or spiritual health? If not, then what is it?

2.  Many people "give up" aspects of their lives without ever intending to do so. Think about the characters in the movie clip. What have they "given up" unintentionally?

3.  If strangers came to your parish, what things would they see or hear that might make them think that Christianity is more about what you don't do than what you do?

4.  Have any of you used Lent as a period of self-denial? If so, what motivated you to do so? If you are not familiar with the idea of lenten self-denial, how does it strike you?

*Brainstorm*                                    (10–15 min.)

5.  Make a list of all the things you can think of that might be beneficial to give up, whether for a short while, a long while or for good.

6.  List all the reasons you can think of why giving up any of those things might be beneficial.

7.  Highlight all items on the list that are beneficial, or at least harmless, if taken in moderation.

---

*View Movie Clip*                                (5 min.)

*Scenes:* Comte taking Serge to confession; catechism class; time passing; the villagers in the confessional; Comte at home, drinking water with lemon.

*Discuss*                                       (5–10 min.)

8.  *Chocolat* is superficially about a battle between giving up food and enjoying chocolate. But what other "if it feels good, do it" behaviors does the film explore?

9.  In your opinion, is Vianne a brave freedom fighter or a sinister and subversive destroyer of traditional values?

---

*Imagine* (10–15 min.)

Recall the two scripture readings from your personal reflection earlier.

10. What would have happened if Jesus had *not* withdrawn to the desert and been tempted for forty days before he began his ministry?

    What would have happened if Peter and Andrew, James and John had *not* given up the security of their employment and followed Jesus?

11. What might have happened if the rich young man *had* given away everything that he owned and embarked on a new life?

    What may have happened to him if he did not?

---

*Meditation* (5 min.)

In some moments of silence, ask God to show you:

➤ anything it might be healthy—mentally, physically or spiritually—for you to give up;

➤ anything you have inadvertently given up that it might be time for you to rediscover.

READER 1: Some words of ancient wisdom from Ecclesiastes 3:1–8.

*Brief pause*

READER 2: Some words of St Paul, grappling with the
ethical issues of his day, from 1 Corinthians 6:12 and
19–20.

**Prayer**

> Father God,
> Who created all things for our delight,
>> help us to live life to the full.
> Teach us never to neglect or refuse
>> the many good things you offer us.
> Teach us to appreciate the simple joys of being
>> human,
>> and teach us, in our turn, to create delight for
>> others.
> But, Lord, keep us alert, lest we start to use your
>> good gifts
> in a way that you never intended.
> Keep us from the overindulgence
>> that turns healthy appetite into addiction.
> Teach us that fruit out of season can be sweet to
>> the lips
> yet poison to the body.
> Strengthen our weak wills and deal with those
>> deep longings
>> that make us crave what is bad for us.

We ask, Lord, for your forgiveness when we fail.
>We acknowledge that it is *when* and not *if*,
>>because each of us is fallible.

We ask you that because of this fallibility we all
>share,
>>you will help us to be gentle with ourselves and
>>with others...as you are with us.

In the name of the demanding, forgiving, prob-
>ing, and gentle Christ. Amen.

## To Continue Your Reflection

It is fascinating to note that fasting is a common factor in all major religions and even among those whose reasons for limiting their food intake are not specifically religious, as the proprietors of health spas and Weight Watchers groups can testify.

Perhaps what we are looking at is a common human urge to strip life back to the basics every once in a while. Perhaps it is an instinctive feeling that in order to be more spiritually aware, there are times when the material things you so depend on just have to go.

Of course, giving up is not just about a healthy body. There are ways in which mind and spirit can be honed and strengthened by times of abstinence, not least from the constant pressures and distractions of our frenetic world. It's good to remember that our well-being is a holistic issue: body, mind, and spirit growing together.

There may come a point, however, when some holistic philosophies part company with the New Testament. Christ's message is inescapable: self-denial is not only about the good it does for *me*. The sort of giving up that works best is that which has a deeper purpose behind it.

In this program, therefore, we are exploring not only "giving up" but also "giving out." If you want to give to others, it will almost always involve giving up something you would rather keep for yourself. Nursing a sick relative involves a loss of time and freedom. Making a charitable donation involves not spending money on something you might otherwise afford. And there are some evils that simply cannot be conquered by remaining uninvolved at a distance. There are times when someone must be willing to give up creature comforts and security and just *go*—live among the world's needy as Jesus did—in order to fully understand and fully serve.

On the one hand, *Chocolat* could easily be seen as an "anti-Lent" movie. But on the other hand, Vianne could be seen as a role model of the kind of self-denial Christ advocated: a person giving up security and status in order to fulfill a calling as a kind of "traveling healer." It is a calling with a cost to Vianne and her daughter, and like all callings, it raises hard questions: "Am I really doing this because I am *called*, or because I am *driven*? And how right is it to impose my own calling on my child?"

"No pain, no gain," say today's fitness instructors. "Count the cost," says Jesus to those who want to build something of their lives. If our calling is a true calling, then it will have a cost worth paying (so long as it is one we choose for ourselves and do not impose on unwilling others).

Another personal confession (not quite so terrible, since I imagine almost everyone reading this book could say the same!): I have lived very comfortably for just about all of my life. I am used to hot water, central heat-ing and a decent mattress, and have no desire to forgo them. I have not yet been a missionary, or an emergency volunteer. Somehow these particular tasks have never come my way. But I say "not yet" because I would like to think that if God ever needs me—to feed refugees, to visit the elderly, or to campaign for change, be it in the Third World, the inner city, or even a French village—I hope that I am not so addicted to security, routine, and comfort that I would be unable to meet the challenge.

I would like to think so, but…

Am I so physically, mentally, and spiritually "flabby" that I am likely to miss the opportunities that God wants to give me?

To be honest, I don't know.

Do you?

---

## Personal Reflection

*Read Luke 5:27–32; 7:36–50.*

Jesus did not prepare himself for ministry in order to make himself some sort of super-spiritual being. He prepared himself for a life among people, all sorts of people. Being where they were, doing what they did. Listening, talking, healing, challenging, risk-taking, absorbing all the criticisms thrown at him. "Giving up" is of limited value if it does not result in "giving out."

### Brief pause for reflection

*Again this is an exercise in imagination, with no right or wrong answers.*

▸ What might have been different, both at that time and in the centuries that followed, if Jesus had refused to attend the tax collector's party or the Pharisee's dinner? And what might this say about the idea of "giving out"?

## WEEK TWO

# Giving Out—
# The Power of a Gift

## To Start Your Reflection

### Pause for Thought

Try to remember times when others have done something or said something that has made you feel loved and accepted.

### The Gift of Encouragement

I am frequently surprised by things that other people remember that I have forgotten completely. "Do you remember," said my very oldest friend recently, "when you and some of the others bought me a pencil case for my eleventh birthday? It was the first time anyone except my immediate family had bought me a present and it meant so much." "I always remember," said another friend, "when you threw a surprise party for my twenty-first birthday." A letter arrived a few months ago. It was from the pastor of a parish we once attended, someone I hadn't seen for twenty years or so, who had just read an article I had written. "I still remember your kindness," he said, "in traveling all the way to see my new home."

I had forgotten all these things. I am not listing them here to tell you what a nice person I am; rather, the opposite! I think God may have sent these little reminders to tell me something else I was in danger of forgetting: that in the long run, little kindnesses may be far more important than running an efficient office or writing successful books.

There are certain other things I remember, though, that are probably long forgotten by the person who did them. The encouraging words spoken by another student in a writing course when I had just nervously shared my first attempts at fiction and was feeling completely out of my depth. The girl at my new job, whom I hardly knew but who bothered to say, "I like your outfit. You always dress so nicely!" I'm not sure it was true, but it made me feel so much better.

A card arrived one day, months after we had moved to a new area, from an old friend who just wanted to say she missed us. It didn't matter that it came so late. God allowed it to come at just the right time when we needed encouragement.

Some other things that frequently take me by surprise:

» The number of times someone who at first glance I thought might be boring or "not my type" turns out to be someone whose company I enjoy.

» The number of times I think I am doing a good turn for someone, only to find that the benefits I receive back far outweigh what I gave.

» The number of times getting to know someone from another country or another culture or with another set of beliefs has enriched me.

---

## Personal Reflection

*Read Luke 14:1–24.*
This parable is often taken to refer to the Jews and Gentiles: God had poured out his generosity on his people, the Jews, but often they had failed to take advantage of it, so now God was offering an invitation to the Gentiles as well. While that may be true, Jesus' forthright comment in verses 12–14 shows that he was not just trying to make a religious point. He meant it—quite shockingly—literally.

## Pause for Thought

» What could you say to encourage someone today?

» How could you show acceptance this week to someone who feels unaccepted?

# Group Encounter

*View Movie Clip*       (10 min.)

*Scenes:* Armande reminiscing, Vianne's gift to Josephine, Vianne visiting Josephine.

*Brainstorm*       (10 min.)

1. For the moment, leave aside any questions you may have about Vianne, her "pagan" influences, her motives, etc., and look just at the good things she does. In this clip, how does she reach out to other people? List all the different things she does and says in this clip that offer people love and acceptance.

2. Cast your mind back to when Vianne first met both Armande and Josephine. How did they behave? List the things they said and did that might well have discouraged her from getting to know them. How would you have reacted to those initial encounters?

3. Hopefully (!) your parish has plenty of people who are prickly, difficult, a bit odd, or socially unacceptable. List all the reactions inside you that might make you avoid them.

*Readings*       (5 min.)

READER 1: Luke 5:27–32

Courtesty of Photofest

*Brief pause for reflection*

READER 2:  Luke 7:36–50

*Brief pause for reflection*

**Ponder and Share**                    (10–20 min.)

Take a few minutes of silence to think about the following questions. Afterwards, if you feel you want to, share your thoughts with the group.

4.  Think about ways in which someone's act of generosity to you—whether of time, respect, listening, a practical gift, showing appreciation for what you had to offer them, etc.—has made a difference to your life.

5.  Are there any people that you first felt uncomfortable with or disliked who have ended up enriching your life?

---

**View Movie Clip**                    (5 min.)

*Scene:* Armande's party.

**Discuss**                    (5–10 min.)

6.  Vianne arranged the party for Armande knowing that the rich food, especially sweet things, could kill

her. Was this the right thing to do? To what extent should we give people what they want, even if we know it is bad for them?

***Ponder and Share***                    (10–20 min.)

One of the greatest gifts we can give to others is our time. Sometimes, what others need most is not counsel or prayer or deep conversation but just time spent having fun. One of the most neglected gifts is the gift of an invitation—to a meal, a walk, a cup of coffee, a movie— it need not be anything grand or elaborate.

Spend a few minutes in silence to think about the following questions before sharing your thoughts.

7. Think of a time when an invitation came as a special gift to you. Do you spend enough time having fun with others? When was the last time you had a good laugh? Does your church community as a whole spend enough time together doing social things (whether formal organized activities or informal ones)?

8. What are the reasons you give for not spending more time having fun? (Such as: "The business of living, earning money, looking after the family, cleaning the house, takes up all my time." Or, "A Christian's mission and purpose is too important to waste time in frivolous things." Or, "I don't have anyone to have fun with.")

9. What are the real reasons you don't take this time? (Such as: "I'm too tired to bother." Or, "I wouldn't know what to do." Or, "I'm afraid of being refused." Or something else?)

---

***Meditation*** (10 min.)

***Begin with a few minutes of silence.***

READER 3: Friendship is fragile and must be approached gently and patiently. The following passage explores this idea. It is taken from *The Little Prince*, a fantasy story by Antoine de Saint-Exupéry about a boy who lives alone on a tiny planet with a rose bush as his only companion. The boy journeys to find other worlds, and on another tiny planet he meets a fox:

> Come and play with me," proposed the little prince, "I am so unhappy."
>
> "I cannot play with you," the fox said, "I am not tamed."
>
> "What does that mean—'tame'...?"
>
> "It is an act too often neglected," said the fox. "It means to establish ties."
>
> "'To establish ties'?"
>
> "Just that," said the fox. "To me you are still nothing more than a little boy who is just like a hundred thousand other little boys. And I have no need of

you. And you, on your part, have no need of me. To you I am nothing more than a fox like a hundred thousand other foxes. But if you tame me, then we shall need each other. To me you will be unique in all the world. To you, I shall be unique in all the world."

"I am beginning to understand," said the little prince. "There is a flower. I think she has tamed me. ..."

"One only understands the things that one tames," said the fox. "Men have no more time to understand anything. They buy things already made at the shop.  But there is no shop anywhere where you can buy friendship, and so men have no friends any more. If you want a friend, tame me."

"What must I do to tame you?" asked the little prince.

"You must be very patient," replied the fox. "First you will sit down a little distance from me—like that—in the grass. I shall look at you out of the corner of my eye and you will say nothing. Words are a source of misunderstandings. But you will sit a little closer to me every day..."

And so the little prince does, and eventually he and the fox become friends. Later the fox explains more:

"It is the time you wasted for your rose that makes your rose so important... Men have forgotten this truth," said the fox. "But you must not forget it. You become responsible for what you have tamed. You are responsible for your rose..."

*Brief pause for reflection*

READER 4: We listen now to a reading from a well-known passage from Paul's letter to the Corinthians—so well-known that the radical nature of its message may have lost the power to shock us: 1 Corinthians 13:1–10.

*Brief pause for reflection*

## Prayer

Teach me to dance
 to the beat of your heart,
Teach me to move
 in the power of your Spirit,
Teach me to walk
 in the light of your presence,
Teach me to dance
 to the beat of your heart.
Teach me to love
 with your heart of compassion,
Teach me to trust
 in the word of your promise,
Teach me to hope
 in the day of your coming,
Teach me to dance
 to the beat of your heart.
Amen.

# To Continue Your Reflection

### The Gift of Hospitality

One thing that disappoints me about the Gospels is that Jesus never gave a party (except perhaps the Last Supper; which was understandably somewhat somber in tone).

But even if he never hosted one, he was a welcome guest at several, spoke of others, and never showed any hint of disapproval no matter how disreputable the company. His followers certainly made it clear that welcoming others into your home was an important factor in following Jesus.

"Practice hospitality," says Paul succinctly to the Roman church (Romans 12:13). "Offer hospitality to one another without grumbling," writes Peter (1 Peter 4:9). The first Christians, according to their chronicler Luke, "broke bread in their homes and ate together with glad and sincere hearts" (Acts 2:46).

In a way, early Christianity did not need to say a great deal about hospitality. When Moses set down the laws of the embryonic Jewish nation by listening to God and recording what he heard, periods of feasting and celebration were put in place as a vital part of the Jewish cycle of life. And of course, entertaining strangers was so ingrained into the Jewish way of life—indeed of all Middle Eastern life, as it is today—that the writer to the

Hebrews needed only to remind them: "Do not forget to entertain strangers, for by so doing some people have entertained angels without knowing it" (Hebrews 13:2). The story of Abraham, who found that the travelers he had invited into his tent were actually messengers from God, was so well-known as not to need naming.

But of the many good things that have been handed on from biblical times into Western Christianity, sadly, hospitality is not always one of them. It sometimes seems that the more we have, the less we are willing to share.

---

## Pause for Thought

➤ What are some of the reasons why you and those you know are sometimes reluctant to invite others into your homes?

*Read John 2:1–11.*

I often wonder how the staunch prohibition supporters of previous times dealt with this one: Jesus' first miracle, used for something as frivolous as providing wine for a party. And not just for the toasts, either! Verse 10 suggests that the celebration was already "somewhat lively" by the time this occurred. Do you think Jesus did this to make a statement, or just to give help when it was needed? Whether it was an intentional statement or not, what messages do you take from this story?

## Pause for Thought

What act of hospitality could you perform in the next few weeks? It need not be anything big, because the aim is not to impress another, but to make someone feel loved and accepted.

## Week Three

# Getting Wise—
# The Possibility of Change

## To Start Your Reflection

### Pause for Thought

What answer would you give to the question: What is the movie *Chocolat* about? Take a few minutes to think about it before reading on.

One thing that has fascinated me as I have discussed this movie is the variety of answers I have heard to the above question. "It's about Lent versus chocolate." "It's about self denial versus self-indulgence." "It's about traditional Christianity versus vaguely spiritual remedies." "It's about tolerance and welcoming strangers." "It's about what you do being more important than what you don't do."

Yes, it is all these things and more, and they will all come up during this program. But I want to turn now to something you may not have thought of. Because I think that at its heart, this movie is about *control*.

The imaginary French town of Lasquenet is like most communities, especially religious ones. There is an unspoken pact between those who control and those who assent to be controlled. It is ruled by habits (be it lenten observance, mistrust of the "river rats" or the widow Audel's protracted mourning) whose original reasons may have been lost in the mists of time. The arrival of Vianne, the stranger who refuses to accept the town's norms, throws everything into confusion.

## Personal Reflection

*Read Matthew 12:1–21.*

## Pause for Thought

Just as the stranger Vianne questioned the "status quo," so it was in first-century Palestine. Only this time the stranger was Jesus, striding across the Judean countryside, ignoring restrictions that had become petty, turning the tables, showing no fear for those who dominated or controlled. Strange then that the Church that bears his name (both Protestant and Catholic) is so often known as the most hierarchical and authoritarian institution around. Strange but true—sadly, there is no shortage of evidence to bear this out.

Playwright Edward Bond, writing in the 1960s, claimed, "God is a secular mechanism, a device of class rule." Before you dismiss that as left-wing rhetoric, it is worth looking at his logic, drawn from the pages of history. He explains that for a long time, the Church's teaching was used to "help enforce acceptance of the social order... To be saved, a man had to accept the church's teaching on the way secular society should be organized... Leaders of church and state often came from the same families."

Fortunately that sort of world—where kings could proclaim themselves head of their own national church and families like the Medicis could produce generations of dukes, cardinals and popes in equal measure—is long gone. Unfortunately, many share Bond's view that the Church hasn't changed since then!

Of course, "authority," "tradition," and "hierarchy" are somewhat demonized words in a postmodern, anti-church culture, and we may need to reclaim for them their rightful place. A society that totally jettisons any authority and tradition is a society without order or common values—a society adrift. An organization with no hierarchy is a confused and inefficient one. The point is that hierarchy should be both flexible and accountable: open to question and open to change.

What most people have a problem with in the Church is *authoritarianism*—authority without the possibility of challenge, authority claimed for the user's own ends.  When this comes into play, as in recent church scandals, then it is easy for the Church as a whole (and even God) to get unjustly tarred with the same brush.

Is it possible for the Church to renew itself with regard to this oppressive image?

Some say that the only way is to dismantle the old structures and create new ones. But new structures are often as full of authoritarianism as the old ones. The traditions are new traditions, that's all. The new authority figure might be someone in a Hawaiian beach shirt rather than a robe, but might be just as controlling.

Others would answer that the only solution is to have no structures at all. "I can be a Christian without going to church." Well, maybe, but the first thing Jesus did was to establish a group of followers and the last thing he did was to ensure it would continue. And humans are social beings. Even if every church were abolished tomorrow, the day after someone would start a club for people who don't go to church anymore and the day after that someone would organize a committee and a set of rules!

Yet others, including a host of postmodern philosophers, would say that the whole thing is impossible anyway. They would draw on Nietzsche's idea that any claim to possess absolute truth is an invalid assertion of power. Anyone who claims to have "capital-T Truth" must be on a power trip. Anyone who believes they know God must be mad, bad, or an oppressor.

It's a tempting argument. Except that Jesus did and he wasn't.

Unfortunately, the world at large doesn't see Jesus...it sees *us*. It is looking at us Christians and evaluating Christianity on what it sees. And what the world sees is not always what we wish to show it.

I believe this issue of control and authority is huge. Recent scandals within the Church, plus the rise of fundamentalism outside it, have created a widespread atmosphere of mistrust of anyone claiming authority in the name of God. There is probably no issue more serious for the Christian church in this century. I also believe that the answer is there, staring us in the face, in the pages of the Gospels. The way for the Church to overcome an oppressive image is simple. We need to look at the words and actions of its founder and let them sink into our lives. Simple, yet radical...and far from easy!

# Group Encounter

*View Movie Clip* (5 min.)

*Scenes:* Beginning of film, under opening credits: in church, wind blows door; Vianne's arrival.

*Discuss* (25–35 min.)

1.  The village of Lasquenet, like many small communities, was locked into tradition. What was good about the traditional way the village functioned?

2.  *Tranquilité* doesn't seem such a bad thing—after all, who doesn't want life to be safe, secure and calm? But what damage is done by this sort of tranquility, this need to maintain an ordered, uncontroversial life at all costs? What unhealthy situations did it lead to in the film?

3.  How would you evaluate your church and/or local community on a "*tranquilité* scale": too much, not enough, just right?

4.  *Chocolat* gives voice to a common view in our society: religion is to be mistrusted because it so often leads to oppression. Clearly this is not what Christ had in mind. Equally clearly, there is ample evidence for this view. So what is it about communities of

faith and their leaders that might make them suscep-
tible to misuse of authority?

5.  What might need to change if Christ turned up at
    your parish or in your community?

---

*View Movie Clip*                                    (5 min.)

*Scene:* Outside shop, Guillaume with dog meets widow
Audel; Comte visits hairdressers; Comte and priest in
graveyard.

*Brainstorm*                                    (15–20 min.)

6.  "If you lived in this village, you understood what
    was expected of you, you knew your place in the
    scheme of things." In the film, who controls and
    who allows themselves to be controlled?

7.  What do we learn from the film about these charac-
    ters' backgrounds that might explain why they be-
    have the way they do?

8.  In the movie, what techniques and tools do the
    "controllers" use to intimidate? In what other ways
    have you experienced intimidation or seen others in-
    timidated?

9.  In the movie, how do those who refuse to be intimi-
    dated demonstrate their defiance? Are there any

other useful ways you have learned to stand up to those who intimidate?

---

*Meditation*                              (10–15 min.)

In silences that follow, ask God to show you any issues of inappropriate control in your life.

READER 1: Matthew 23:1–12, 23–28.

*Brief pause for reflection*

READER 2: When the north wind blows the church door open, the Comte de Reynaud is quick to shut it. Does he even notice the searing light outside? Does he think of anything other than keeping his world safe and contained, keeping things the way he feels they should be?

*Brief pause for reflection*

When Vianne, the mysterious stranger, comes to the village, she knocks on a door. If she is welcomed, it may change everything.

*Brief pause for reflection*

When Christ, in John's vision in Revelation, spoke to a church that was comfortable and safe, he said this:

"Those whom I love, I rebuke and discipline. So be earnest, and repent. Here I am! I stand at the door and knock. If anyone hears my voice and opens the door; I will come in and eat with him and he with me" (3:19–20).

*Brief pause for reflection*

Christ also said: "I have come that they may have life, and have it to the full" (John 10:10).

*Brief pause for reflection*

## Prayer

Lord,
Help us to open the door—to allow the wind of the Spirit to blow through our stuffy lives.
Help us to open the door—to welcome strangers and intruders who may just be Christ in disguise.
Help us to open the door—to changes and disturbances that may just have something to teach us.
Help us, Lord, to open the door to you.
Amen.

# To Continue Your Reflection

During the writing of this book, my eye fell on an old newspaper put on the bathroom floor as protection while the room was being decorated. Since our family lives in the real world rather than that of TV's Trading Spaces, it had been there for some time. The paper was dated a few days after the dramatic events of September 11, 2001, and it showed a cartoon of Bush and Blair trying to look Churchillian. The speech box above their heads said, "We shall not flag or fail. We shall go on to the end. We shall fight somebody or other on the beaches, in the fields and on the hills of somewhere or other... We shall never surrender."

Whether or not subsequent events have born that out, I shall leave you to decide. The point is that under the circumstances, it was an understandable knee-jerk reaction.

When our tranquility is threatened, our first thought is usually to try to regain control. And in order to do that we feel we need an enemy. We feel we need something or someone to fight, and the temptation is not to look too closely at whether or not the blame really lies there or whether or not fighting will solve the problem. The point is that we want to find an enemy that is external. The last thing we want to do if we are feeling insecure is to admit that some of the problem might possibly lie within.

The Comte de Reynaud knew this. He was no fool, says the film's narrator, and he knew that even if he achieved the drunken Serge's rehabilitation, that alone would not be enough for him to regain control of the town. "Some greater problem needed to be identified and solved." And of course, conveniently, the river rats came sailing up the river and gave him the enemy without.

*Read Matthew 23:1–12, 23–28.*

Since he was a twelve year old visiting the Temple, Jesus had observed the religious leaders of his day. He had seen them struggling to hold on to their authority in a society where the power was held by a conquering army with quite different gods. Jesus saw not just the absurd lengths to which this need for control led them, but what the essential problem was. Some of them thought that if they could sort out the externals, then the internal would be solved too. Jesus knew that it had to be the other way around—they had to clean the inside first.

And Jesus had something even more radical to say. If you really wanted to change things, then the solution lay not in trying to hold on to control, but in voluntarily giving it away. It lay in being a servant.

Dangerous ideas. And ones that made Jesus himself immediately become the "enemy without."

**Pause for Thought**

» Who or what do you see as "the enemy without" in your life?

» Is it possible that this outer enemy, this problem, may really lie within yourself? Can you name it?

» Is it even a problem to which it is possible to attach blame?

### Week Four

# Getting Real—
# The Power of Acceptance

## To Start Your Reflection

### Accepting Difference

There was a time when North America was mostly Christian. By that I don't mean that everyone was moral and pious and worshipped regularly. Rather, if someone was moral, pious, and worshipful, it was most likely within a Christian framework. Whether you lived within its boundaries or without, Christianity was the most prevalent religion.

Now it is different. There are substantial numbers of people in our countries who believe quite different things from us. We cannot share the same cities without respecting them. And we can, and often do, fly off to other continents and find ourselves immersed in societies utterly different from us in their beliefs, their customs, their attitudes.

The result? We have made the "shocking discovery" that it is possible to be moral, pious, and worshipful without being Christian! Not only are we exposed to other religions, but to those who embrace beliefs, practices, and spirituality outside the framework of any organized religion at all. A myriad of remedies, therapies, and cosmologies are on offer, and Christians are sharply divided in their reactions to them. There are those who feel that anything that comes labeled as an "alternative spirituality" must be demonic. Others believe that at worst these alternatives are misguided and at best helpful tools in the Christian quest for the spiritual.

Recently I visited Kuala Lumpur. In the middle of this teeming, cosmopolitan Muslim capital was something very odd—a row of mock-Tudor villas 'round a cricket green. It was, of course, where the British lived and ruled back in colonial days, and you can find similar "outposts of the British empire" all around the globe. You may also find more contemporary variants in places like Spain's Costa del Sol with its "Red Lion pubs" and fish-and-chip shops. This is one way of living with difference, albeit detrimental: retreating into your own tight "expatriate" community, clinging to your traditions and becoming an "us" carefully insulated from "them."

To be a minority is threatening. And to be a minority in matters of belief is even more threatening. Belief is fragile by nature. It deals with things that cannot be seen or touched or proven. And it is precious and personal, at the center of our being. We would be strange believers, then, if we never felt threatened by those whose beliefs were different from ours. To feel threatened by difference is a natural reaction. It is what we do with those threatened feelings that matters.

Dealing with difference is never easy. But deal with it we must, or the Church will gradually retreat into a world of unreality. (There are some who say this has already happened!) It is doubly difficult where issues of faith are concerned, because they have to be dealt with on two levels. On one level there is the objective evaluation of the belief or practice itself. Is it untrue, or simply a different way of saying the same thing? Is it harmful, or just unfamiliar?

And on another level there is the need to deal with our threatened feelings. How can I evaluate a belief or practice objectively when it raises so many uncomfortable questions within me? Even if I believe this practice is wrong, how am I going to love and respect the person who practices it?

At root perhaps, the question revolves not around what we believe in, but whom. If we have learned to trust a loving God, who not only made but infuses the whole of life, if we have learned to follow in the footsteps of a humble, forgiving Christ—then very little can threaten us. (And in those moments when we still feel intimidated, we have someone to help us through it.) Secure in our own faith commitment, we can begin to celebrate and explore difference rather than fear it. We can embrace those of other faiths without losing our own.

## Pause for Reflection

*Read John 4:4–26.*

Jesus was not afraid to talk to someone from a different ethnic and religious group—and a woman of dubious morals, to boot! When he started getting too close for comfort on personal matters, she was quick to divert him onto more general religious controversy (a common technique). Jesus did not ignore the controversy or give way on his belief, but he was quick to turn it around to the essence of the matter: what was important was not *where* you worshipped or *what* you did, but *how* you did it.

## Pause for Thought

Of those from other faith traditions whom you have met, whom have you found the most threatening and why?

# Group Encounter

*View Movie Clip* (5 min.)

*Scene:* Vianne tells Anouk the story of her grandparents.

*Discuss* (10–15 min.)

1. In the chocolaterie, there are several things that spread an air of mystery: the spinning plate, the hint of secret ingredients, Vianne's "I know your favorite" approach. Do you think these are just a game, a clever marketing ploy, or do they have more sinister undertones? If the latter what makes you think so?

2. How do you react to Vianne's "pagan" roots? Do they make you feel curious or uncomfortable? If you met her or someone like her would you want to know more or would you back off?

3. When you meet someone with a religion or belief system other than your own, do you first notice similarities or differences? Why?

*Ponder and Share* (10–15 min.)

Take a little time in silence to think about any experiences you have had with other religions or alternative therapies, or even with different branches of Christianity. Share your reactions to that experience:

4. What are the things that have made you feel uncomfortable about them?

5. What have you learned from them?

*Brainstorm* (10 min.)

6. On your board/sheet of paper, draw two columns: "Attractive" and "Off-putting." Put yourself in the place of someone in today's society, someone without a faith of his or her own, "shopping around" to find something to believe in and somewhere to belong. Imagine yourself in this person's shoes (maybe you can think of someone you know) as he or she visits different churches, explores other faiths, or tries out alternative therapies.

   Then under each column write down the things you might encounter in the people who belong to these various groups, the way they practice their faith, the way they behave towards you, and the dynamics of the group. What might entice you to get involved or might put you off?

## Optional extra question

7. Go through with a highlighter pen and mark those that apply to your church in particular.

*View Movie Clip*                  (5 min.)

*Scene:* Vianne and Armande in the chocolaterie; Vianne meeting Roux : "I'd like to apologize"; Serge apologizing to Josephine; the public meeting.

*Ponder and Share*             (10–15 min.)

8.   Have you ever "helped someone to understand they were not welcome"? It may not be as reprehensible as it sounds; chances are that you have had to do so for one reason or another. If so, why? Is there a way of doing so that still respects the person's dignity?

## Optional extra question

9.   Josephine accepted Serge's apology, but she refused to return with him. Was she right to do so?

*Brainstorm*                 (10–15 min.)

Roux (the river rat), with long experience on the margins of society, expects that people are either going to either accuse him, or try and save him: "Which idea are you selling?" If we have any real belief in the Christian message, then it follows (doesn't it?) that we believe it can save people and therefore we do want to share it.

10. What conditions can we put in place to ensure that we share our faith in a positive and not a negative

way? Make a list of attitudes that encourage faith sharing that is appropriate as well as effective.

---

*Meditation*                              (5–10 min.)

READER 1: Mark 12:28–31.

*Ponder in silence*

Why do you think that Jesus put loving God as the first commandment? After all, most of his teaching was supremely down to earth. Might he not have said that the most effective way to show your love for God *was* to love your neighbor? Is there anything about the process—about being in right relationship with God *first*—that enables you then to relate to your neighbor with a more loving attitude?

READER 2: St. Francis of Assisi is said to have told his followers: "Go preach the gospel. Use words if necessary."

*Brief pause for reflection*

READER 3: The following reading shows how radical and revolutionary the gospel is. When truly practiced, it will be quite evident even without words: Matthew 5:43–8.

*Brief pause for reflection*

**Prayer**

> Lord,
> We acknowledge that who we are speaks much
>     louder
>     than what we say, or even what we do.
> Help us to accept ourselves fully
>     as God accepts us,
> So that we may accept others fully
>     as God accepts them.
> Help us to forgive ourselves fully
>     as God forgives us,
> So that we may forgive others fully
>     as a token of the forgiveness God wants them
>     to receive.
> And help us to be quicker to celebrate difference
>     than to condemn it.
> In the name of the loving, forgiving, accepting
>     Christ.
> Amen.

## To Continue Your Reflection

*Read Matthew 5:43–48.*

What on earth does Jesus mean by that last statement in this passage, "Be perfect"? To be honest, I'm not sure. (And I don't think I've ever come across anyone else who really knew, either.) But I think I can be pretty certain, based on the other things Jesus said and did, about two things it doesn't mean.

*It doesn't mean that only people with an unblemished record can get into the kingdom of God.* Jesus made it clear that he had come not for the righteous, but for sinners. He made it clear that God the Father welcomed back prodigals. He told the criminal on the neighboring cross, "I tell you the truth, this day you will be with me in paradise" (Luke 23:43).

*It doesn't mean that anyone is even likely to achieve perfection.* Jesus' model prayer makes that clear: "Forgive us our sins, as we forgive everyone who sins against us. And lead us not into temptation" (Luke 11:3–4). He told the religious leaders of the day that for all their law keeping they were like "whitewashed tombs" (Matthew 23:27). He said that prayer was not about telling God how good we were, but about asking mercy for our sins (Luke 18:9–13).

So why did he say "Be perfect"? Was he brainstorming? Did the gospel records get it wrong? As I said, I'm not sure. But one thing I have discovered: these outrageous, unexpected sayings of Jesus have an immense value, because what they do is stop us in our tracks and make us think.

If it's impossible to be perfect, then why advocate it? Well, maybe to make it unequivocally clear that living life God's way is not about achieving a passing mark. There is no "70 percent needed for a passing grade, 95 percent for distinction." It just doesn't work like that.

And thank goodness it doesn't. For if it did, we would be forever evaluating how well we were doing, trying to gain "brownie points," checking our grade average. We would be forever looking inwards.

*Read Mark 12:28–31.*

The essence of a perfect life, as Jesus makes supremely clear, is about looking upwards and looking outwards.

Yes, there is some looking inwards to be done. Because as Jesus also makes clear we are to "love our neighbors *as ourselves.*" In those two words, Jesus demonstrated that he understood, centuries before Freud and Jung had drawn breath, what whole libraries of psychology and self-help books have tried to say since: that in order to love and accept others, you need to love and accept yourself. And to do this you need to know yourself as one who is forgiven.

This is where the circle returns to the beginning. Because in order to love and understand ourselves, in order to love and understand others, we need to know unequivocally that none of us is perfect.

None of us lives our lives with perfect wisdom and compassion. None of us *never* tires or becomes fed up with our nearest and dearest. None of us fulfills our potential. None of us has a perfect grasp of the truth.

Years ago, my father said something that stuck in my mind. He remarked that if we did meet someone perfect, we'd never recognize it. I think he was probably right. Because when it comes to it, we have a pretty odd idea of what perfect is. We expect the physique of Michelangelo's David, the brains of Einstein, the charm of Princess Diana, the compassion of Mother Teresa. We make an assumption that perfect people would be good at everything, that their bodies and their behavior would conform to some norm of beauty. Perfection would mean perfect conformity. And so, not surprisingly, we all secretly feel that if we did meet someone perfect, we would instantly dislike her or him.

I think, though, that what my dad was trying to say was that perfection would mean being perfectly and wholly yourself, quite unique in how you looked and what you did and thought and said. (I have since discovered that the original Greek word for "perfection" used in this verse has more to do with maturity and fulfillment than with being unblemished.)

I don't think any of us totally achieves this maturity. I suspect, though, that the ones who come nearest to it are those who would never in a million years imagine themselves to be so. Those who are so accepting of themselves—of their gifts and strengths and of their flaws and failures—that they can happily get on with looking upwards and outwards without thinking about it. I suspect that the ones who come nearest to perfection are not the ones we envy most, but the ones who most make us feel good about ourselves.

And I bet, although I have no theological evidence to support this, that if we did meet someone perfect, one earmark would be his or her ability to laugh at himself.

**Pause for Thought**

As you go about your daily life this week, look around you for those who may be nearer to perfection than you had ever suspected.

## Week Five

# Growing Up—
# The Process of Change

### To Start Your Reflection

For a few minutes, take an imaginary journey with me and with some of the characters of *Chocolat*.

Picture Paul de Reynaud as a chubby seven year old in dress shirt and tie, with hair slicked down, ready for mass. "One day you will be Comte de Reynaud," his mother tells him, "and upon you the moral welfare of this village will rest." Picture him passing by the statue of his ancestor in the square every day and seeing that steely gaze of responsibility falling, it seems, on him alone.

Picture Josephine, a teenager giggling as the boys pass by, full of dreams for the future. Watch as it gradually dawns on her that her father is a collaborator with the hated Nazis. See her shame as the Germans withdraw from France and her father is dragged into the square to be spat upon and beaten. Picture her, forever tainted, her dreams dashed, reaching out for some sparkling jewel left behind in a bombed house. Just for a moment, the glitter stills the ache in her heart.

Picture Caroline, a gawky eleven year old in the high school gym. "Sorry," says her new friend, "my mom says I can't come over after school." Caroline knows why. She knows what they say about her mother. Armande Voisin, the sleaze. She swears, reads dirty books, drinks with the men, does no housework. Worst of all, she says exactly what she thinks. "When I am older," vows Caroline, "I'll never put my children through this."

Picture nine-year-old Vianne on yet another rattling bus, journeying to yet another unknown town. "It's fun," her mother tells her. "We're not like those other people. We are wanderers. This is our life." See Vianne as she presses her nose to the glass and conjures up that ever-dimmer memory of the man who seemed so kind and gentle: her father, one of those "other" people. "Yes, maman," says Vianne. "It's going to be fun."

When we are small children, our parents seem like God to us. As we grow, we discover they are sometimes wrong. By the time we are teenagers, we usually think they are wrong about everything! But still, they leave with us an immense heritage of ideas, attitudes, and emotions—things so deeply ingrained that we never question them. Indeed, we probably don't even know they are there, until one day something or someone comes along to challenge them.

There are two ways of dealing with this subconscious legacy. One is to try and dig it all up. Bring it all to the surface and examine every bit of it. The other is to keep it all deeply buried. To push it down, to cover it over, the moment it threatens to pierce the surface.

The first way—counseling or therapy—is helpful but costly, in time and probably in money. There may be times when it becomes a desperate necessity in our lives. And yet, even as you reap dividends in terms of increased self-knowledge, you run the risk of being exposed to things you are not yet equipped to deal with (which is the reason that professional help is so important).

The second way—repression—is less than helpful, and still likely to be costly, certainly in terms of mental well-being and quite possibly in terms of physical health. Its "benefit" is that on the surface, things keep running smoothly; indeed, there are times when life is just too demanding for prolonged introspection. But it can be rather like tiptoeing around a minefield. If you don't know what is buried where, then you never know when something is likely to explode.

Thankfully, as I have gone on in my faith life, I have discovered that these two are not the only alternatives for coping with what life has dealt us. If you have entrusted your life into God's hands, then I believe he will often allow your hidden attitudes and emotions to surface one by one at just the right time, at a time when you are ready to deal with them.

Of course, it will never *feel* like the right time. It will never *feel* comfortable and cozy when the deepest things about us are challenged. That's why trusting God is so important at these times, making it possible to welcome those challenging intruders as friends rather than resenting them as enemies, because you are no longer facing them alone. If you are committed to growth, if you are learning to trust God as a loving parent who wants only good things for his children, then it at least becomes possible to ride those feelings, to "hang in there," and to trust that God is a specialist in bringing strength out of weakness and joy out of pain.

## Pause for Reflection

*Read John 3:1–8; Matthew 18:1–3.*

These readings can provoke many thoughts and be interpreted in many ways, but one thing Jesus seems to be saying is that it is possible to begin again. No, we cannot enter again into our mother's womb. We may not be able to undo our parenting and our background or culture, but we can release its harmful hold on us. We can become new people. We can see the world through childlike eyes again. It is not only possible, Jesus implies, but *necessary*. To be fully the people God wants us to be, we have to take off our adult straitjacket and become willing to learn.

### Pause for Thought

Ask God whether there is anything from your past that is quite near the surface right now and ready to be dealt with. Perhaps you will need to look at your present tensions, reactions, and emotions and ask yourself if they have their roots in something from your past. If something comes to mind, look at it for a while, but then commit it into God's hands. Ask God to deal with any shame or blame, and to show you also what strengths and blessings your past has given you.

# Group Encounter

*View Movie Clip* (5 min.)

*Scene:* Caroline mends the bike; Armande's funeral; Vianne drawn by mother's ashes; Caroline and Comte, "No one would think less of you..."

*Brainstorm* (10 min.)

Many of the characters in *Chocolat* "grow up" in the course of the film. But in order to do so, they have to acknowledge their need to change.

1.  Which characters "grew up" in the movie, and what did they have to acknowledge in order for the process of change to start?

2.  What was the point at which this process of change began for each of them?

3.  And then, what action did they each take to demonstrate change?

4.  For many of these characters, change required them to step out from under some inappropriate control over their lives. Who did this and who were the controlling characters whose influence they needed to shake off?

*Discuss*                                    (10–15 min.)

READER 1: John 8:1–11

Jesus pointed out only the difference between this woman and her accusers: she had broken the "eleventh commandment": *thou shall not get caught*. Her shame was public while her accusers' sins remained private.

5.  How do you react when you hear that someone "respectable" has a shameful secret? Think about some famous people whose secrets have come to light. How do you react to them? Is there a difference and if so, why?

6.  How have you reacted when someone you knew admitted his or her failure or weakness to you? Has it strengthened or weakened your relationship? Has it strengthened or weakened your respect for him or her?

---

*Ponder and Share*                           (10–15 min.)

READER 2: John 13:37–38; 18:25–27

READER 3: John 21:15–19

Jesus made it clear that failure did not mean you had no future. Perhaps he knew that failure and shame could be as much a means of grace and growth as the most wonderful blessing.

7. Take some time to think about any occasions in your life when you feel you failed, or when you had to admit your weakness in front of others. In what way has that experience made you a stronger or better person?

8. You may like to look at the question from another perspective: think about a time when you grew most: in responsibility, in courage, in spiritual stature, etc. What precipitated that change? Did the growth come from strength or from weakness?

   After a few moments of silence, and if you feel you can, share your thoughts in small groups.

---

*View Movie Clip*                                                     (5 min.)

*Scene:* Pere Henri's sermon; festival; Vianne throws ashes away. In this clip, look out for images that could have some Christian symbolism.

*Discuss*                                                        (10–15 min.)

9. Did you notice any images with close links to Christian symbolism? If so, what were they? What might these have to say to us about our own process of growth?

   Christian doctrine states that Christ was the Son of God and the Son of Man, fully human and fully divine. However, since that is an almost impossible concept to comprehend, most Christians tend to focus on one or the other.

10. Do you think that you as an individual, or you as a church, tend to focus more on Christ's divinity or on his humanity?

11. What difference would it make if the balance shifted? Are there any dangers in going too far one way or the other?

---

*Meditation*                                                (5 min.)

*Brief pause for reflection*

In silence, think back over the whole of this "lenten program." Note the things that keep recurring to you. (Perhaps note also the things you would rather not think about!)

*Brief pause for reflection*

Ask God to show you if there are any lessons you need to learn or put into practice, or any ways in which you need to grow.

---

## Prayer

Lord our Lord,
Whose full divinity was seen in your full humanity,
Send the wind of your Spirit to stir us to change,
Send the fire of your Spirit to lighten our spirits,
Send the dove of your Spirit to help us be at peace
   with ourselves.
Take our weaknesses and turn them into
   opportunities.
Take our shame and use it to make us strong.
Help us to be fully human
That in being fully who you made us to be, the
   divine might enter in.
In the name of the mysterious, provoking, healing
   and affirming Christ.
Amen.

### Share

In small groups, share briefly something that you have learned from this lenten program and intend to take away with you. Still in small groups, take a few moments to pray for each other, either aloud or in silence.

## To Continue Your Reflection

### Lighten Up

When I came to write these concluding words, I asked myself: "What message has preparing this lenten program left with me? What message would I most like people to take away with them?" The answer that came into my head and lodged itself there, somewhat unexpectedly, was this: "Lighten up."

*Oh sure!* I hear you say. *Haven't we just been talking about change and growth, and confronting subconscious attitudes and inappropriate control, and loving our neighbor and self-denial? Not exactly lightweight. And aren't we approaching Holy Week, with Jesus on the cross and pain and blood and death and sin and all that?*

All true.

But it seems to me that the picture *Chocolat* paints of church is a place full of gray, guilty, burdened people, straitjacketed by convention. In contrast, Vianne's chocolaterie was a place of welcome and ease. It was a place people were *listened to* rather than *talked at*. It was a place of acceptance and lightheartedness. And because of that, it was a place where people blossomed.

Church, too, can be a place where people blossom. I have seen it happen—many, many times. Discovering that God loves you and accepts you is the most wonderful, liberating experience you could possibly have, and Christians often form the most loving and caring community it is possible to find.

Just one warning though: I have sometimes seen these same people go on to wilt under the pressure of what they feel they now ought to become. This is rarely an intentional pressure, but can sometimes be the received message—usually in the form of a steady drip of "Should do better" from the pulpit!

I believe that Jesus intended his followers to be joined together, that God wants Christians to be community and that we can serve the world better together than we could apart. But I also think that very many Christians need to "lighten up."

At its core, Christianity is about relieving guilt, not inducing it. It's about easing burdens, not piling them on. It's a message that Jesus gave very clearly and one that has been built into the very fabric of the Church itself. Repentance and confession form an integral part of our worship—not to make us feel guilty, but so that the experience of guilt that is part of being human can be exchanged for the forgiveness that is at the heart of the nature of God. The Eucharist Celebration is intended to be a gift, not a duty!

A couple of years ago I attended Eucharist at Salisbury Cathedral. It just happened that I had seen the movie *Billy Elliot* the night before. The cathedral's atmosphere inspired me—the deep harmonies of the or-

gan echoing around ancient stone, the exquisite choir
voices soaring up to the magnificent arched ceiling, the
glow of light through stained glass. When it came time
for receiving communion, I looked at us: solid, respectable and middle-aged, approaching the altar stiffly and
reverently with lowered eyes. And it seemed almost...
unfitting.

We should have been tap-dancing down that long
aisle, running and leaping and twirling and kicking like
Billy Elliot! There should have been a jazz band and
trumpets and a chorus of angels jiving above us! Because
what we were actually celebrating was so amazing. God
loves us. Enough to die for us. Jesus gives himself to us
as nourishment and wants us to be free and strong and
forgiven! (No, I didn't start tap-dancing—but maybe
it's not too late to learn!)

*Read Matthew 11:28–30.*
These three verses have been haunting me for months.
What does it mean to take on Christ's yoke? What can I
learn from him about living under a *light* yoke?
Here are just a few thoughts on the subject:

» We are designed for activity and work.

» But Christ does not intend us to live weary, burdened lives.

» Therefore we need to learn a new, lighter way of being as we go about our daily tasks.

- This does not mean being naïve, because we need to resist being manipulated by others.

- But the trick is discerning what we believe Christ wants of us.

- The secret is being gentle and humble of heart.

- Living humbly for Christ relieves us of the burden of always having to "get it right."

I don't think I've yet discovered all these scripture verses have to tell me, but I'm still looking. Perhaps you too would benefit from reading and rereading this simple appeal from Jesus, letting it sink into you until you begin to grasp what it means to live under his light yoke.

When I first led the part of the program in week two that talks about having fun, someone said to me, "But you haven't mentioned joy." No, I didn't, because you can't manufacture joy. You can create fun, you can create welcome, you can create pleasure, but you can't create joy. Joy is a by-product. Telling Christians they *ought* to be joyful is about as silly as telling newborn babies they *ought* to be able to talk.

But you can, I believe, create an environment that allows joy to flourish. I think both the movie *Chocolat* and the words of the Gospels have some clues on how to do that. I hope that as you go on to celebrate Easter, you will have begun to catch a glimpse of what this joy might mean.

# Postscript

Priest and writer Gerard W. Hughes describes "the longest and most difficult journey in the world" as "the journey from the top layer of our minds to the heart."

What he means is that it is relatively easy to mentally embrace an idea, but not at all easy to incorporate it into the depths of your being, to the place of your gut reactions, to how you live.

It may be that there are things in this lenten program that have provoked you to think. You may have considered ideas that you would like to take further. (It may also happen that this impulse will have drifted out of your consciousness even before you step out the door once the last session is done!)

This would hardly be surprising. If you had been a Christian 150 years ago, it is quite likely that the only intellectual stimulation you had from week to week would have been at church. No television, no internet, no phone, e-mails, junk mail, radio, films...maybe a personal letter or two, maybe the odd book or newspaper, but nothing like the quantity of words and images that bombard us daily in the twenty-first century. Indeed, you probably would have worked at some manual labor—scrubbing the laundry, ploughing the fields, hauling coal, piecework in a factory—work that gave you plenty of time to contemplate and digest the ideas that *did* come your way. Whether that was a better or worse lifestyle than today's is beside the point. It was different…vastly different.

While it is true that a large amount of the words and images that are thrown at us today are junk—junk mail, junk TV, junk films, junk novels—an awful lot is not. As a writer, I know that while ours can be a rewarding profession, it is also extremely tough. You would not put yourself through this roller-coaster existence unless you had something to say about what it means to be human. Admittedly, the result may have been pummeled or squeezed or stretched by the "forces of Mammon" in the process, but the chances are that much of what you see on the screen or read in print came originally from the depths of someone's experience and therefore has the potential to speak deeply to you. Even if the hymns you sing or the preaching you hear lack a certain intellectual rigor or spiritual profundity, they are usually based on scripture verses that possess those qualities. You can always go back to the source!

I hope that if this lenten program has done nothing else, it may have convinced you that God can speak to you through movies. God can speak through anything or anyone, of course, but movies are a very potent medium, and ironically, the "forces of Mammon" collude to make it so. The financial resources and human effort needed to make a film is so great that you simply don't embark on a film project unless you think that many people will want to see it. And since there is only so much you can do with sex and violence and special effects, Hollywood is hungry for stories that engage the human spirit. And good stories, by their nature, are about conflict and journey and change and what it means to be human. Their conclusions may not be Christian, but in provoking us to thought and debate, they can provoke God's thoughts in us.

So, how can we ensure that these thoughts take the long journey from the top of our head to the depths of our being?

One thing I'm sure Gerard W. Hughes would endorse is that it takes time. Time apart from the bombardment of words and images that we experience today on a daily basis. Quiet time. Time perhaps when the rhythm of physical exercise or labor stills our mind and allows us to listen.

Another help may be writing things down. Keep a journal of what you read and see and hear. Note the things that seem like God speaking to you. Note also the things that perplex you or confuse you or irritate you. Revisit your journal occasionally and see whether any of those things have begun the downward journey to your heart.

I practice these things imperfectly myself, but I can say with honesty that they work. But then, admittedly, I am both a writer and an introvert. I like writing things down. I like being alone. If these things are not for you (but don't be too quick to decide that they are not), then another discipline that may speed the journey from mind to heart may be simply to speak out. Share the ideas that are stirring in you with someone you trust. Ask him or her to back you up in prayer and to come back to you and inquire on your progress.

How you do it doesn't matter, but above all, embark on the journey. (To help you get going, I have added some questions below.) It may seem that I am just advocating more things to fit into your already complicated life. But I am convinced that, curiously, taking time to contemplate and sift your thoughts will lighten things up rather than add to your burdens. Because if you know clearly in your own heart what things God wants you to do, then it becomes a whole lot easier to sift through all those other demands when they come crashing in.

It is better to hear one word from God and to incorporate it into your being than to hear hundreds and thousands of wise words that only ever get as far as the top of your head.

Jesus had some succinct and witty comments on the subject, and I can do no better than end with these:

> Therefore everyone who hears these words of mine and puts them into practice is like a wise man who

built his house on a rock. The rain came down, the streams rose, and the winds blew and beat about that house; yet it did not fall, because it had its foundations on the rock.

But everyone who hears these words of mine and does not put them into practice is like a foolish man who built his house on sand. The rain came down, the streams rose, and the winds blew and beat against that house, and it fell with a great crash. *(Matthew 7:24–27)*

## Pause for thought

‣ What things, if any, have arisen from this program that I need to think about further?

‣ What things, if any, have arisen from this program that I don't want to think about?

‣ What things, if any, have arisen from this program that irritate or confuse me?

‣ What things, if any, have arisen from this program that I need to try and put into practice?

# Leader's Notes

## Before you begin

### Previewing the Movie

The program runs for five sessions, but I strongly recommend that all program participants see the whole movie beforehand. Even if they have seen it some time previously, a viewing just before the program to refresh their memories is important. I suggest, therefore, organizing an introductory session before the program starts in order to view the movie.

### Obtaining a Viewing License

To obtain the license to show *Chocolat* in a public setting, contact:

> Swank Motion Pictures, Inc.
> 201 S. Jefferson Avenue
> St. Louis, Missouri 63103-2579
> 800-876-5577

# Using Movie Clips

### For Video-VHS

The timings I have given for the excerpts used are based on the assumption that the VCR is set to zero at the opening of the film, i.e., when the words "Miramax Films Present" comes up against a black background. (This is after the Miramax logo.)

If you do not have a minutes and seconds counter on your VCR, you will need to work out the "In" and "Out" points for yourself, based on your own machine's counter. Even if you do have a real time counter, it might be well to double-check the timings on your own machine. In my experience there seem to be slight variations, especially when fast-forwarding.

Make sure that the movie is set up and ready for the first clip before the session begins. The second clip is trickier, but try to get as near as you can just by using the counter, without fast-forwarding on screen. Try to practice this beforehand to avoid disrupting the meeting too much by cueing back and forth. If you are really a technical klutz like me and find this too difficult, then settle on using only one of the clips during the session, and describe the action and quote the script for the other.

### For DVD

Scenes from the DVD are found quite easily by using the chapter selection feature that is available through the

DVD menu. Using the chapter selection, just choose the chapter provided and play that scene. Once in the scene, scan forward until you reach the times I have provided in minutes and seconds. The minutes and seconds will be displayed on the face of your DVD player or the screen when scanning.

## Knowing the Movie

As I said in the general introduction, you as leader might do well to see the film through at least twice beforehand, in order to really absorb its detail and nuances. You will probably need to familiarize yourself with the character names (see p. xiii) and it may even be helpful to the whole group to have them written up on a board for general reference. However, to help you further, I have given some "prompt answers" in the leader's notes for that session to cover any points you may have missed.

## Knowing Your Group

I have tried to make the group outlines as user friendly as possible, but please feel free to adapt as needed for your particular group. You will probably find that in groups larger than six or eight, discussion might be difficult, or at least some people will find it harder to take part. You will notice there is a minimum and maximum time for each activity. Keeping to the minimum time will give you an approximate one-hour session, while using the maximum times will result in the session lasting an hour and a half. However, these are suggestions, feel free to follow the Spirit's lead and adjust to your group's needs and desires.

## Setting the Boundaries

It may be wise, certainly at the beginning of the whole program and perhaps at the beginning of every session, to refer to the boundaries needed to create a "safe sharing environment" (p. xiv): *confidentiality, respect,* and *genuine listening.* It may also be worth repeating the definition of community (p. xv). As there is so much material in these sessions, it may be important to ask that each person keep his or her contributions fairly brief.

Within these sessions there is the potential to deviate onto other topics: other faith traditions, alternative therapies or beliefs, sharing your faith, others' view of the church, etc. This program is much more about individual, personal reactions and growth than about beliefs and organized structures. However, it may well provoke issues that ideally could be followed up at a later date. Make a note of these and, if appropriate, refer the group to the *References and Resources* section at the back of the book, which suggests some ideas for further reading.

## Addressing Deeper Issues

It became apparent during some of the trial sessions of the program that some questions were touching on deep issues in people's lives. One member very wisely suggested that it was important not to raise painful or difficult matters and then leave them hanging in midair. Out of this came the suggestion that time for individual prayer could be offered at the end of each meeting, should anyone need it.

Although it will probably be too late at the end of an evening meeting to spend more than a very short time in prayer, it may be an opening for further listening, befriending, and prayer to take place at a later time. Be sure to have resources available if it becomes apparent that someone might benefit from professional counseling.

## Throwing a Party

At the end of the trial run of this program, our group decided it would be fun to hold a *Chocolat* party. It took the form of a chocolate feast: a three-course meal with all three courses containing chocolate! You might think that that was unbearably rich and unpalatable, but in fact, with high cocoa-content chocolate used sparingly, it was delicious, and we had such a good time that it began to convince me there might be something to the argument that chocolate is a "mind-altering substance" after all!

In our case, it was just a fun ending to the program, but if, during the series, some of the discussions about hospitality and welcoming strangers have taken root, you might like to follow them up by using it as a way of inviting others to join your circle of friends.

The feast could even be an Easter celebration—and I have a hunch that Jesus himself might be delighted to join the party! (See p. 129, "Ideas for a Chocolate Feast.")

# WEEK ONE

## Giving Up—A Prelude to Change

*Show Movie Clip*     (5 min.)

*In:* Just after Caroline's line, "mistake…I just told you that you made one"; farmhouse at night.

> *15 min. 20 sec. for VHS.*
> *Chap. 5; 1 min. 12 sec. for DVD.*

*Out:* Back view of three widows walking down road.

> *18 min. 42 sec. for VHS.*
> *Chap. 6; 2 min. 29 sec. for DVD.*

*Discussion*     (20–30 min.)

Depending on the number of participants, you may want to either have a discussion all together, or divide into groups and allocate one or two questions to each group. (If you divide into groups, then use 10–20 minutes in groups and leave 10 minutes for sharing your group's insights with the rest.)

## Question Prompts

There is no prompt for question number 1.

2.  One thing that is worth pointing out is how drab these people's lives are. They have given up trying to brighten up their lives.

3.  Think about the quality of the community's participation in the liturgies: where do the emphases lie? Think also about visual impressions, both of the liturgical environment and of the people who participate. Think about what is missing as well as what is present.

There is no prompt for question number 4.

*Brainstorm*                                           (10–15 min.)

There are no question prompts for questions 5–7.

You will need a large pad of paper, a felt-tip pen, and a highlighter pen for this.

In a rapid-fire session, think of as many answers to the following questions as you can. Try to encourage people to contribute answers as quickly and spontaneously as possible.

Elect someone as "scribe" to take down the answers and if possible display them on a board or on a large, pinned-up sheet of paper.

---

*Show Movie Clip*                                      (5 min.)

*In:* Comte and Serge crossing the village square.

> *45 min. 39 sec. for VHS.*
>
> *Chap. 10; 3 min. 9 sec. for DVD.*

*Out:* "…some greater problem needed to be identified and solved."

> *49 min. 50 sec. for VHS.*
>
> *Chap. 11; 00 min. 29 sec. for DVD.*

*Discussion*                                    (5–10 min.)

## Question Prompts

There is no prompt for question number 8.

9. People may have strong opinions on this and it might be necessary to stress that there are no "right answers." Or perhaps that the right answer is not "either/or" but "both/and."

*Imagine*                                       (10–15 min.)

This is an exercise in imagination; there is no "right answer" to these questions. Hopefully, group members will have read the scripture passages and thought about the questions beforehand. If this has not happened, then the group leader may need to give an explanatory introduction to each gospel incident. So be sure you are familiar enough with the passages to explain the incidents in question.

10. Scripture citation is Matthew 4:1–11, 18–22.

11. Scripture citation is Mark 10:17–27.

---

### *Meditation*                                    (5 min.)

Be sure to ask participants to be readers ahead of time and determine how you will prompt them to begin, so that the prayerful atmosphere is not disrupted.

### Prayer

After the second reading is completed, allow 3–5 minutes of silence, then invite the group to pray the prayer together, using "Let us pray" or another invitation.

> *Note: Don't forget to suggest that if the session has brought anything up that people would like to talk about or pray over, they can approach parish leaders or someone else they trust at the end.*

## WEEK TWO

# Giving Out—The Power of a Gift

*Show Movie Clip*      (10 min.)

*(It might be better to read Question 1 below together before showing the clip.)*

***In:*** Just after Anouk at school: "You don't have a father." "Sure I do, we just don't know who he is." First words: Armande: "I was out all night with him..."

*24 min. 52 sec. for VHS.*

*Chap. 7; 5 min. 00 sec. for DVD.*

Play to the point where Vianne leaves the bar and Josephine smells the chocolate in her hands.

*29 min. 24 sec. for VHS.*

*Chap. 7; 8 min. 41 sec. for DVD.*

Then if preferred fast forward through the scenes where Luke sketches the bird and Vianne goes to see the Comte. Come back in for Vianne greeting Josephine outside shop. "How long have you been standing here?"

*32 min. 30 sec. for VHS*

*Chap. 8; 3 min. 05 sec. for DVD.*

***Out:*** Josephine: "You make the most wonderful chocolate."

*35 min. 05 sec. for VHS.*

*Chap. 8; 5 min. 45 sec. for DVD.*

*Brainstorm*                                    (10 min.)

You will need a large pad of paper, a felt tip-pen, and a highlighter pen.

In a rapid-fire session, think of as many answers to the following questions as you can. Try to encourage people to contribute answers as quickly and spontaneously as possible.

Elect someone as "scribe" to take down the answers and if possible display them on a board or on a large, pinned-up sheet of paper.

## Question Prompts

1.  Ways in which Vianne offers love and acceptance:

    ‣ She gives Armande the gift of listening.

    ‣ She is interested enough to ask about Armande's needs: "You have a problem?"

    ‣ She gives Josephine a gift of chocolates (despite knowing she has stolen?).

    ‣ She actively seeks out Josephine and refuses to be put off by Serge.

    ‣ She indicates that she understands Josephine's kleptomania but still accepts her: "I know."

    ‣ She asks Josephine's advice: "Do me a favor, try one of these rose creams."

    ‣ She stops and looks at Luc's drawing and praises it.

- She doesn't try to tell Josephine where she is wrong: "No, I don't think you're stupid."

- She respects Josephine enough to accept her point of view, even though she realizes it is wrong: "Then it must be true, my mistake."

2. Off-putting ways in which Armande and Josephine behaved:

   - When Vianne first turns up at Armande's, she is greeted rudely, "Who the hell are you?"

   - Despite the terrible condition of the old patisserie, Armande stomps off, telling Vianne to keep it in good condition.

   - When Armande first comes to the chocolaterie, she is rude and abrupt.

   - When Josephine first comes in, she steals, is unfriendly and mutters to herself. She has previously been glimpsed outside the window and been described as "waltzing to her own tune."

   - When Vianne visits Josephine, she is not welcoming: "What do you want?"... "I don't have friends. Does Serge know you're here?" (Also, Serge's reaction to Vianne's visit might put her off getting involved with Josephine.) Josephine shows fear at the visit, both fear of Serge and fear of the Comte. It might be worth pointing out that we learn later that the Comte owns the bar and they are just tenants.

3.   Reactions to difficult people might include:

» fear;

» anger, irritation, annoyance;

» they seem to highlight your own failings;

» embarrassment: not knowing what to say or how to deal with them;

» concern that if you are seen to be friends with socially unacceptable people, you might become socially unacceptable yourself.

*Readings*             (5 min.)

Ask two participants to be readers ahead of time.

*Ponder and Share:*       (10–20 min.)

There are no prompts for questions 4 and 5.

If your group is large, you may prefer to divide into smaller groups. Read the two question aloud and let the group know how much time they will have to reflect quietly. Then, let the participants know when it is time to share their reflections.

*Show Movie Clip*       (5 min.)

*In:* Armande dressed up in her party hat (just after food preparation, wind starts to blow, chocolate being stirred).

> *1 hr. 12 min. 57 sec. for VHS.*
> *Chap. 15; 00 min. 00 sec. for DVD.*

*Out:* Caroline arrives on riverbank to see them dancing on boat.

> *1 hr. 17 min. 15 sec. for VHS.*
> *Chap. 15; 4 min. 34 sec. for DVD.*

*Discuss*                                        (5–10 min.)

No prompt for question number 6.

"Vianne arranged the party for Armande, knowing that it could kill her. Was this the right thing to do?" NB: This is clearly a big issue, and within the context of this meeting there will only be time to provoke brief thought and discussion, rather than reaching solid conclusions. If anyone is interested in pursuing it further, then refer them to a pastoral counselor who can provide assistance.

*Ponder and Share*                              (10–20 min.)

There are no prompts for questions 7–9.

If your group is large, you may prefer to divide into smaller groups. Read the two question aloud, and let the group know how much time they will have to reflect quietly. Then, let the participants know when it is time to share their reflections.

*Meditation:* (10 min.)

Ask two participants to be readers ahead of time.

## Prayer

After the second reading is completed, allow 3–5 minutes of silence, then invite the group to pray the prayer together, using "Let us pray" or another invitation.

> *Note: Don't forget to suggest that if the session has brought anything up that people would like to talk about or pray over, they can approach parish leaders or someone else they trust at the end.*

## WEEK THREE

# Getting Wise—The Possibility of Change

*Show Movie Clip*                                        (5 min.)

*In:* Just before narration begins: "Once upon a time…"
   *1 min. 06 sec. for VHS.*
   *Chap. 1; 1 min. 41 sec. for DVD.*

*Out:* Just after Vianne knocks on the door.
   *4 min. 34 sec. for VHS.*
   *Chap 2; 00 min. 06 sec. for DVD.*

*Discussion*                                        (25–35 min.)

### Question Prompts

There are no prompts for questions 1–3, 5.

4. I used the phrase "communities of faith" because I wanted to widen it to all religious groups, not just churches, but perhaps it is the "faith" aspect rather than the "communities" that is more important in this consideration.

   ‣ Try and tease out what it is about *spiritual* authority that makes it different, e.g., a priest, by his various functions, takes on a role as mediator between God and humanity. It is very easy therefore

WEEK THREE

to view the priest in a "god" role generally. A preacher may tell his or her flock that "God says..." and therefore takes on the role of mouthpiece of God.

▸ This may be valid in, for instance, a straight quote from Scripture, but it may also be a way of manipulating the congregation into certain actions or viewpoints. And because Christians so much want their church to reflect the kingdom of God, they can be very reluctant to question, expose malpractice, or rock the boat in any way.

### *Show Movie Clip*                                   (5 min.)

*In:* Widows looking in shop window.
   *18 min. 13 sec. for VHS.*
   *Chap 6; 2 min. 00 sec. for DVD.*

*Out:* Just after: "important to know one's enemy."
   *22 min. 17 sec. for VHS.*
   *Chap 7; 2 min. 14 sec. for DVD.*

### *Brainstorm*                                    (15–20 min.)

You will need a large pad of paper, a felt-tip pen, and a highlighter pen.

In a rapid-fire session, think of as many answers to the following questions as you can. Try to encourage people to contribute answers as quickly and spontaneously as possible.

Elect someone as "scribe" to take down the answers and if possible display them on a board or on a large, pinned-up sheet of paper.

## Question Prompts

*Note: In each of the following four questions, I have tried to include every possible answer I could think of. However, don't feel you have to extract every one of them from the group or run through them all yourself. Use as appropriate.*

6. Who allows themselves to be controlled?

   ‣ Parishioners
   ‣ Pere Henri
   ‣ Josephine
   ‣ Anouk
   ‣ Luc

*Who controls?*

   ‣ Comte de Reynaud
   ‣ Serge
   ‣ Vianne
   ‣ Caroline, Luc's mother

WEEK THREE

7.  Clues from the characters' backgrounds:

*Comte:*

> ‣ His shame at his wife leaving him leads him to divert attention by looking for shame and blame in other situations (and perhaps the free-and-easy Vianne reminds him of his wife).

> ‣ He bears the weight of his heritage. He has probably been told that he should live up to his illustrious ancestors and has been brought up to think of himself as guardian of the town's morals.

*Caroline:*

> ‣ Her mother Armande tells Vianne that Caroline never used to be so protective of the boy before her husband died. She is terrified of losing her son and mother as she has previously lost her husband (presumably to illness).

*Josephine:*

> ‣ Serge tells the Comte that Josephine's father was a collaborator with the Germans and that no one else would have her. Josephine has been brought up to live with shame.

*Serge:*

> ‣ The scene in the catechism class shows us that Serge is none too bright and possibly illiterate.

Perhaps that is why he has turned to violence as a way of proving himself.

8. Techniques which the controllers use to intimidate:

*Comte:*

- We are shown that he is the landlord for both the hairdressers and the bar (and presumably also for other places in the village), so he has economic power over the villagers.

- He plays on Pere Henri's youth and inexperience, insists on correcting his sermons, and uses the example of the previous long-serving priest to intimidate him.

- He uses Pere Henri's sermons to play on the parishioners' sense of guilt and religious fear: "Satan has many guises... for what could seem more harmless than chocolate?"

- He is not above a well-placed, slanderous bit of gossip. In the hairdressers: "My heart goes out to that poor illegitimate child of hers."

- He plays on people's social fears in trying to get rid of the "river rats:" "These people... would contaminate the spirit of our quiet town, the innocence of our children..."

*Serge:*

- Physical violence.

*Vianne and Caroline:*

> ‣ Parents of course have a right and a duty to control their children. The problem lies in doing it in the child's best interest and in knowing how to permit more freedom gradually as the child gets older.

9.  Demonstrations of defiance:

*Pere Henri:*

> ‣ Eventually seizes the opportunity to deliver the sermon he wants to preach.

*Josephine:*

> ‣ Leaves Serge.
> ‣ Hits him over the head with the skillet.
> ‣ Refuses to go back.

*Luc:*

> ‣ Meets Armande, his grandmother, at the chocolaterie.
> ‣ Goes to Armande's party.

*Anouk:*

> ‣ Fights against moving on again.

*Vianne:*

> ‣ Makes it clear she does not conform to the Comte's values: tells him right away that she is unmarried and doesn't go to church.

‣ As soon as difficulties arise, goes to see the Comte and confronts him.

‣ Makes a point of buying jewellery from Roux the river rat when she knows the Comte is watching.

‣ Organizes Armande's party.

‣ Organizes the Easter festival.

---

### *Meditation* (10–15 min.)

Be sure to ask participants to be readers ahead of time and determine how you will prompt them to begin, so that the prayerful atmosphere is not disrupted.

### Prayer

After the second reading is completed, allow three to five minutes of silence, then invite the group to pray the prayer together, using "Let us pray" or another invitation.

> *Note: Don't forget to suggest that if the session has brought anything up that people would like to talk about or pray over, they can approach parish leaders or someone else they trust at the end.*

**WEEK FOUR**

## Getting Real—The Power of Acceptance

*Show Movie Clip* (5 min.)

*In:* Vianne and Anouk in bed, just after "You make the most wonderful chocolate."

   *35 min. 08 sec. for VHS.*
   *Chap. 9; 00 min. 00 sec. for DVD.*

*Out:* Just after Vianne: "Goodnight, mama."

   *38 min. 45 sec. for VHS.*
   *Chap. 9; 3 min. 34 sec. for DVD.*

*Discussion* (10–15 min.)

You may like to divide into smaller groups for both this session and the following *Ponder and Share*. If so, come back together and allow five to ten minutes at the end of the combined session to share conclusions from each group.

### Question Prompts

There is no prompt for question 1.

2. The *Encarta* dictionary defines "pagan" as "somebody who does not follow one of the world's main religions. The *Chambers* dictionary defines it as "one who has no religion, one who sets a high value

on sensual pleasures." It is perhaps also worth considering that "pagan" when used to describe a religion, is referring to something *pre*-Christian rather than necessarily *anti*-Christian.

There is no prompt for question number 3.

***Ponder and Share***                          (10–15 min.)

***Brainstorm***                                  (10 min.)

There are no prompts for questions 4–7.

4–6. Note that I have said "different branches of Christianity" and "different churches." People within your group are likely to have come across a wide range of experiences, as will people trying to find out about the Christian faith. Try and keep the questions broad to reflect them all.

***Show Movie Clip***                             (5 min.)

***In:*** Boats going up river, Anouk watching, just after children playing on banks and child calls, "Hey, look."
> *50 min. 08 sec. for VHS.*
> *Chap. 11; 00 min. 50 sec. for DVD.*

***Out:*** Just after Comte says in village meeting, "...but we can help them to understand they are not welcome."
> *56 min. 27 sec. for VHS.*
> *Chap. 11; 7 min. 26 sec. for DVD.*

*Ponder and Share* (10–15 min.)

## Question Prompts

8. "Helping someone understand they are not welcome" may be necessary in a wide range of situations: you may have had to deal with an employee who is lazy or unsuitable, a tenant who is impossible to live with, a friend or classmate of your child who is disrespectful or unruly. It may be necessary in a church service if someone becomes disruptive, or even in a prayer group, if someone is so difficult or dominant that it ruins the whole group.

There is no prompt for question number 9.

*Brainstorm* (10–15 min.)

10. If people in your group have experience of any organizational "mission" situations, then it might be worth discussing what safeguards need to be put in place within that organization to ensure that the sharing of faith is done appropriately, e.g. training sessions, necessary parental consent, whether service should be given unconditionally or with evangelical strings attached, etc.

*Meditation*                    (5–10 min.)

Be sure to ask participants to be readers ahead of time and determine how you will prompt them to begin, so that the prayerful atmosphere is not disrupted.

## Prayer

After the last reading is completed, the leader allows three to five minutes of silence, and then invites the group to pray the prayer together, using "Let us pray" or another invitation.

---

Be aware that this session may have touched on all sorts of issues regarding different beliefs or practices. Make a note of any particular issues within the group and follow up if possible by suggesting appropriate reading material or follow-up sessions to explore the issue concerned. See p. 137, *References and Resources*, for some recommended reading.

*Note: Don't forget to suggest that if the session has brought anything up that people would like to talk about or pray over, they can approach parish leaders or someone else they trust at the end.*

WEEK FOUR

## WEEK FIVE

## Maturing—The Process of Change

***Show Movie Clip***                                          (5 min.)

***In:*** Caroline in yard with bike, just after Roux says goodbye to Vianne, "I know. I'm sorry. I'm sorry."

   *1 hr. 29 min. 45 sec. for VHS.*
   *Chap. 17; 2 min. 26 sec. for DVD.*

***Out:*** Just after Caroline says, "Goodnight, Paul."

   *1 hr. 34 min. 14 sec. for VHS.*
   *Chap. 18; 2 min. 39 sec. for DVD.*

***Brainstorm***                                          (10 min.)

### Question Prompts

This session will probably work best by taking a character at a time and going through all four questions before moving on to the next character. Below is a list of the main characters and their stages of growth.

*Caroline:*

1. Needs to acknowledge that her fear of loss is making her overprotective towards her son.

2. Seeing Luc enjoying himself dancing on the boat becomes a catalyst for change.

3. She demonstrates change by fixing up the bike for him to ride and by challenging the Comte about his wife's absence.

4. She needs to shake off the Comte's control.

*Luc:*

1. Needs to acknowledge his own worth and the fact that he is a person in his own right.

2. Meeting his grandmother becomes a point of change.

3. He demonstrates change by continuing to see his grandmother secretly and by going to her party.

4. He needs to address his mother's tight protectiveness.

*Josephine:*

1. Acknowledges to Vianne her stealing and the fact that she is being beaten.

2. Vianne actively seeking her out and expressing her acceptance becomes a catalyst for change.

3. She takes action by leaving her drunken husband Serge.

4. She needs to step out from under Serge's control.

*Comte:*

1. Needs to acknowledge the dangers of his control over others; that his wife isn't coming back; his own

weakness. Before the cross, he says, "All my efforts have been for nothing."

2. Change begins when he sees that Serge set the boats on fire, in response to what he thought the Comte wanted, and when he tastes the chocolate.

3. He shows his change by attending Vianne's festival.

4. He probably needs to shake off the expectations that have been put on him by his ancestry.

*Pere Henri:*

1. Needs to acknowledge that the Comte's control is inappropriate and that he needs to assert his own ideas.

2. Change probably only begins when he finds the Comte in the chocolaterie and he seizes his opportunity to gain the upper hand. You can see it beginning to assert itself during Armande's funeral, where he is clearly unhappy with what he has been given to say.

3. He demonstrates change by preaching a sermon from his own heart.

4. He shakes off the Comte's control.

*Vianne:*

1. Has to acknowledge, to Roux the river rat, that Anouk actually hates traveling from town to town. Perhaps has to acknowledge, following Josephine's

insistence, that her moving on is not only in response to the wind, but could also be running away.

2.  The point at which she spills the ashes and then discovers the people in the kitchen preparing for the festival becomes the point at which she changes.

3.  She demonstrates change by throwing her mother's ashes to the winds.

4.  She has to shake off her mother's controlling influence.

There is also change in other minor characters:

➼ Guillaume Blerot, the elderly gentleman with Charlie the dog, and the Widow Audel;

➼ the Marceaux, the couple whose love life is reawakened;

➼ possibly Roux in that he returns at the end of the film;

➼ possibly Anouk in that she begins to resist her mother's demands to move on.

However, these do not demonstrate the process of change in the same way, and are probably not worth pursuing.

*Discussion*                                         (10–15 min.)

Ask a participant to read the scripture quotation.

### Question Prompts

5. The main point I am expecting to draw from this is that people generally feel more sympathy towards people who admit their weaknesses than toward those who continue to deny and hide them. However, the questions are bound to provoke a mixed response and that is fine.

6. Although I am anticipating that relationships will often have been strengthened by revelations of weakness, there may well be very mixed reactions and responses to this question. It is important to allow space for these mixed responses. The admission of weaknesses is a complex affair, both for those who admit them and for those who listen.

*Ponder and Share*                    (10–15 min.)

7. Again, many people's experience is that they have been strengthened by weakness or failure, but there may well be very mixed responses to this question. Allow them space and look out for any responses that may need follow up prayer or counseling.

There is no prompt for question number 8.

Ask two participants to read the scripture quotations.

You may want to divide into smaller groups for this *Ponder and Share*.

---

***Show Movie Clip*** (5 min.)

***In:*** In church, just after Comte is found in shop window, "I'll think of something."

*1 hr. 45 min. 40 sec. for VHS.*

*Chap. 20; 5 min. 57 sec. for DVD.*

***Out:*** After Vianne throws ashes: "the north wind got weary and went on its way."

*1 hr. 50 min. 07 sec. for VHS.*

*Chap 21; 4 min. 24 sec. for DVD.*

***Discussion*** (10–15 min.)

## Question Prompts

9. The images I had in mind were the twirling woman in white with "wings," who could evoke ideas of an angel or of a white dove, and the man blowing fire. Another, of course, is the recurring image of the wind.

   ‣ All of these are symbols of the Holy Spirit for Christians, and it is perhaps worth touching briefly on the idea that not only does the Holy

Spirit often stir up change in us, but is also available to us to help us through that process of change. In the film, of course, the images are not used in any Christian sense. However, they are not there by accident, but as a way of expressing the release of the human spirit.

10. One aspect that might shed light on this discussion is the songs you sing in your liturgies. Ask yourself how these relate to the Jesus of the Gospels. In our trial group discussions, people identified various types of songs that they felt did not quite mirror Jesus, the actual person we read about:

- the saccharine: "I'll sing a love song to Jesus"
- the warlike: "In heavenly armour, we'll conquer the land"
- the idealistic: "I wanna see Jesus lifted high, a banner that flies across this land…"

However, be aware that people react very differently. Each of these was also someone else's favorite!

*There is no prompt for question number 11.*

---

*Meditation*                                (5 min.)

Read aloud the questions for personal meditation, allowing some time for silence between them.

## Prayer

After 3–5 more minutes of silence, invite the group to pray the prayer together, using "Let us pray" or another invitation.

> *Note: At the conclusion of the program, it might be well to ask of the participants whether there are any unresolved questions or issues any group members feel they want to take further. Again, offer an opportunity to pray over or discuss anything the program has brought up.*

WEEK FIVE

# The Curious History
# of Chocolate

It is fascinating to see how the story of *Chocolat* has its roots in the real-life history of chocolate. As always, truth is stranger than fiction.

## Chocolate and Ritual

For native South Americans, chocolate has always had religious and ritualistic significance. Even today, one of the remnant Maya tribes still prepares two kinds of chocolate drinks, one for their own consumption and one for offering to the gods.

The production of chocolate (or cacao, as it should more properly be called in its original form) began with the Maya, although when the Spanish discovered the New World, it was the use of cacao by the Aztecs that was documented. At the time the beans were used as currency, a custom that continued among poorer people right up until 150 years ago. According to sixteenth-century writings, a slave was worth one hundred cacao beans, while a rabbit was worth around ten.

Chocolate was frequently used in Aztec and Maya rituals and banquets. It was mixed into a liquid used to "baptize" young boys and girls, and the cacao pods were given as offerings to the gods. (Not for nothing was the cacao plant classified with the Latin name *Theobroma cacao*—"the food of the gods!") Chocolate drinks also had a role in marriage and betrothal ceremonies, much like today's champagne. The Aztecs believed that cacao was of divine origin and that drinking chocolate gave mortals some of the god Quetzalcoatl's wisdom. In Aztec society it was seen very much as a drink for the upper echelons— lords and nobility, rich merchants, and warriors.

## Chocolate and Class Structure

When chocolate reached Europe, this practice of chocolate as a drink for the upper classes continued. It arrived during the Renaissance, but it was in the Baroque age that its popularity spread, radiating out from Spain to Italy and, of course, France, where over the centuries prominent chocolate enthusiasts included Cardinal Richelieu, Louis XIV, Voltaire and the Marquis de Sade.

The drinking of chocolate (and drinking it was, because chocolate as confectionery did not appear until the early nineteenth century) was a ritualistic part of aristocratic life, with the whipping up of foam by means of a wooden swizzle stick called a *molinillo,* all part of the tradition.

In the Catholic lands of France, Spain, and Italy, included in these top ranks of society were the clergy. Jesuits particularly became partial to chocolate, even becoming traders themselves. Chocolate never quite caught on in the same way in Protestant England, arriving along with tea and coffee in the 1650s, when Cromwell's puritanical rule discouraged such luxuries. It never gained quite as much popularity as its competitors and was never such an upper class prerogative. Indeed, it was said that chocolate was southern, Catholic, and aristocratic, while coffee was northern, Protestant and middle class.

## Chocolate and the Church

Despite this, chocolate and Catholicism have often had an uneasy relationship.

The question of whether chocolate broke an ecclesiastical fast was a perennial one. Drinks were allowed, but did chocolate merely quench the thirst or did it provide sustenance as well? The arguments raged for two and a half centuries, and at least seven popes made pronouncements on it, all agreeing that chocolate drinks did not break the lenten fast.

Nevertheless, more rigid priests continued to stir up the debate, occasionally bringing in the equally perennial argument of chocolate as an aphrodisiac, "exciting the [physical] appetite." However, stories that a young Peruvian saint, Rose of Lima, was presented with a cup of chocolate by an angel after a particularly taxing session of prayer and visions, did wonders for the pro-chocolate lobby.

Even so, in 1650 the Society of Jesus in the New World issued an act prohibiting Jesuits from drinking chocolate. Embarrassingly, they were forced to rescind it when many of their students started leaving because of the ban.

The story of *Chocolat* is not the first instance of feisty women coming up against the religious establishment. In the seventeenth century in the South American colonial city of Chiapa Real, the upper-class Spanish ladies claimed to suffer from such weak stomachs that they could not get through a cathedral service without taking a cup of hot chocolate. Their Indian maids would bustle in during Mass to serve them, so exasperating the bishop that he threatened to excommunicate anyone who ate or drank during the celebration. In protest, the ladies withdrew to attend Mass at the local convent.

Soon afterwards, the bishop drank a cup of chocolate himself and quickly became ill and died. Through the ages, chocolate has always had a reputation as a favorite vehicle for poison, being particularly effective at disguising it. This unfortunate bishop had apparently suffered the fate of being poisoned by one of his disgruntled flock!

## Chocolate and the March of Progress

As the demand for chocolate grew in Europe, its production changed. Thus it was that cacao groves were planted in the West Indies and the hulls of the three-way trade ships began to be filled with slaves from Africa to labor at their harvesting.

At that time, chocolate was still used mainly as a drink, and just occasionally as a flavoring for food. But in 1828, a Dutch chemist named Van Houten discovered a process for manufacturing powdered chocolate with a low fat content. "Cocoa" had been born. The progression to the modern-day chocolate bar was continued by an English Quaker dynasty, the Fry family of Bristol, who found a way to mix this cocoa powder with other ingredients to form chocolate that could be molded into shapes.

Their rivals, the Cadburys in Birmingham and the Rowntrees in York, also Quakers, were quick to take up the challenge and the great British consumption of chocolate began. At least these Quaker firms had a social conscience, with the Cadburys and the Rowntrees building model towns, most notably Bourneville, for their workers, and the Frys fighting for improved conditions of plantation workers.

The next leap forward in chocolate production was with the Swiss, when Henri Nestlé created milk chocolate in 1867. When Milton Hershey started his chocolate empire in Pennsylvania in 1893, the commercial potential of chocolate knew no bounds.

Of course, as chocolate gradually became big business, so it also bore less and less resemblance to its original form, with sugar, vegetable fats and milk powder often far outweighing the actual cacao content. Today's chocoholics could in fact be sugar addicts.

## Chocolate: Good or Bad for You?

Throughout its long history, opinions have been divided as to whether or not eating chocolate is good for you. Even back in Baroque times, it was claimed on the one hand to promote nervousness and on the other to help digestion.

Present-day scientific opinion varies just as wildly. On the minus side, chocolate, like its early competitors tea and coffee, contains alkaloids—in the case of chocolate, caffeine and theobromine. These alkaloids stimulate the central nervous system and are therefore claimed to cause tension and insomnia. Caffeine, the stronger of these two alkaloids, is known to be addictive, producing withdrawal symptoms of extreme headache. However, cocoa contains much less caffeine than coffee or even tea.

On the plus side, some doctors claim it to be an antidepressant, interacting with female hormones to produce incredible premenstrual cravings for chocolate. A survey by French doctor Hervé Robert, published in 1990, found that the caffeine, theobromine, serotonin, and phenylethylamine contained in chocolate make it a tonic and an anti-stress agent, enhancing pleasurable activities, including making love.

Love is an area in which the reputation of chocolate has been strangely consistent. It has been touted as an aphrodisiac right down the centuries from the Aztec empire to *Chocolat* the movie. In 1662 a Dr. Stubbe reported "The mighty lover Casanova found the drink as useful…to seduction as champagne." Whether there is any evidence for this or for any other of chocolate's claimed physical effects, will no doubt continue to be researched and debated. But on the grounds of "a little of what you fancy does you good," chocolate looks like it's here to stay.

## The Unfair Economics of Chocolate

In recent years, there have been several shocking exposés claiming near slavery conditions of those who work at the supply end of the cocoa industry.

These have eventually provoked action and, on October 1, 2001, a protocol was signed in which the U.S. cocoa and chocolate industry agreed to eliminate child slavery from the chocolate industry. It also "recognized as a matter of urgency, the need to end slavery, serfdom and debt bondage in the growing and processing of West African cocoa beans." The truth is, however, that no one really has clear evidence of how prevalent these types of labor exploitation are. The first large-scale survey is now being undertaken by the International Institute for Tropical Agriculture, surveying three thousand farms across West Africa.

"Child slavery" in the cocoa industry has hit the headlines and it certainly does exist, but probably not as much as in other Third World industries, because the production of cocoa tends to demand strength and skills that children do not have.

Moreover, 90 percent of the chocolate we eat is not grown on huge plantations but on smallholdings—family farms or village cooperatives, where preventing children from taking part could have an adverse effect rather than a positive one.

The most oppressive slavery frequently occurs in the form of bonded labor where someone, on being obliged to take out a loan for a basic necessity such as medicine for a child, is then forced into working for the supplier of the loan, often long hours for seven days a week with only basic food and shelter as payment. Sometimes the loan can never be repaid and is passed from generation to generation. Several sharp drops in the cocoa market in recent years have forced this end result on many farmers.

Ultimately, the real issue is the price paid for cocoa. Even with fairly traded chocolate, the cocoa farmer only gets around 3.9 percent of the price of a bar, with the supermarket getting 34.1 percent, the overheads of production and other ingredients eating up 36.8 percent, the trading company getting 10.4 percent and the government 14.8 percent in taxes. And this is in a chocolate bar that actually contains a significant amount of cocoa—55 percent—as opposed to the 20 percent of most popular chocolate bars. From a typical milk chocolate bar from one of the giant companies, a Ghanaian farmer can expect to see just eight cents from a $1.40 chocolate bar.

So if you want to make difference in the lives of at least some of the fourteen million people involved in the cocoa industry, then make sure that when you do buy chocolate, you choose one of the growing number of fair trade chocolate products now available. See the list below for brands available in North America.

Such products ensure that as much profit as possible go to the people who matter, often by working directly with them. The Day Chocolate Company in the U.K., for example, has made the cocoa farmers shareholders in the company. The farmers have set up an organization, called Kuapa Kokoo in Ghanaian, which operates a credit union and buys agricultural tools at bulk purchasing rates, passing savings on to the farmers. Village co-operatives that perform particularly well are awarded prizes such as machetes or gum boots for use by the whole community. More importantly, the scheme gives the farmers a chance to have a say in how the chocolate is produced and sold, as well as a share of the profits.

Imagine if all the people reading this book decided to purchase fair trade chocolate, and made a point of letting their local supermarket know they would like to buy it, if it is not readily available. Yes, our purchasing power is just a drop in the ocean compared to the might of Nestlé or Hershey. But the story of *Chocolat* demonstrates that even when the existing power structures seem unshakeable, just one person who sticks to their guns can make a difference.

**Chocolate Products Fairly Traded and Available in North America (look for the following brands):**

> Clif Bar
> Cloud Nine
> Dagoba Organic Chocolate
> Denman Island Chocolate
> Gardners Candies
> Green and Black's
> Kailua Candy Company
> Koppers Chocolate
> L.A. Burdick Chocolates
> La Siembre
> Montezuma's Chocolates
> Newman's Own Organics
> Omanhene Cocoa Bean Company
> Rapunzel Pure Organics
> The Endangered Species Chocolate Company

To buy fair trade products online go to,
www.equalexchange.com.

For resources on slavery in the chocolate industry
go to, www.globalexchange.org/cocoa.

More general information on labor abuses can
be found on the web site of Anti-Slavery International,
www.antislavery.org/.

# Ideas for a
# Chocolate Feast

When one of our lenten groups did this, we invited everyone to come wearing something to represent their favorite chocolate, either a name or flavor, and cryptic clues were welcome. Guessing everyone's favorites then proved an enjoyable ice-breaker. You could have dancing or party games after the feast, but we found people were quite happy just to chat.

---

## Suggested Menu

### Appetizer

Fresh Fruit with Semi-sweet Chocolate Ganache

### Main course

Mole Poblano—Spicy Chicken with Chocolate

or

Beef with Balsamic Vinegar and Chocolate

Served with Plain Rice and Mixed Vegetables

## Dessert

*(Recipes for chocolate desserts are legion, but the following has a sharp taste which complements the chocolate)*

Pineapple and Chocolate Cheesecake

---

# Recipes

### Semi-sweet Chocolate Ganache

*(serves 12 generously)*

*Ingredients:*

1 cup heavy cream

1 oz. unsalted butter

1 oz. superfine granulated sugar

12 oz. plain chocolate

*Directions:*

1. Heat the heavy cream, butter and sugar in a large saucepan over medium high heat, stirring regularly. Bring the mixture gently to a boil.

2. Break the chocolate into 1-inch pieces and place in a heat-proof bowl; pour the boiling cream mixture over it and allow to stand for five minutes. Stir until

smooth. Allow to cool for another ten minutes and serve when it is still slightly warm and not too solid.

3.  Serve with a platter of fresh fruit: grapes, sliced apple, banana, orange, kiwi fruit, melon, strawberries, etc.

---

### Mole Poblano

*(serves 12)*

*A festive dish from Mexico, traditionally made with turkey, but adapted here with chicken.*

**Ingredients:**

> 3 large onions
>
> 6 cloves garlic
>
> 4 tbsp. cooking oil
>
> 3 red peppers
>
> 3 lb. boneless chicken breast or stir-fry chicken
>
> 8 oz. raisins
>
> 3 14-oz. cans chopped tomatoes
>
> 2 slices white bread
>
> 8 oz. chopped nuts
>
> 6 oz. sesame seeds
>
> $\frac{1}{2}$ tsp. star anise

3 tsp. chili pepper (or to taste)

$\frac{1}{2}$ tsp. ground allspice

$\frac{1}{2}$ tsp. ground coriander

2 chicken boullion cubes dissolved in 3 cups water

6 oz. dark bitter chocolate

salt and freshly ground black pepper

Fresh coriander or parsley to garnish

**Directions:**

1. Peel and chop the onion and garlic.

2. Trim, de-seed, and chop the peppers.

3. Tear the bread into small pieces.

4. Cut the chicken into 1-inch cubes, and fry in 2 tablespoons oil until brown. Drain and place in casserole dish.

5. While the chicken is cooking, put the onion, garlic, peppers, raisins, tomatoes, and bread into a food processor and blend to a paste.

6. Add the chopped nuts, 4 ounces sesame seeds, and spices, and sauté the paste in the remainder of the oil for about five minutes. Transfer to the casserole.

7. Add the chicken boullion to the pan, together with the chocolate broken into small pieces. Bring gently to a boil until the chocolate has melted, then add to

the casserole and stir thoroughly. Check for seasoning and add salt and pepper as needed.

8. Cover dish and cook for half an hour at 450 F.

9. To serve, sprinkle with chopped coriander or parsley and the remaining sesame seeds, lightly toasted.

---

## Beef with Balsamic Vinegar and Chocolate

*(serves 12)*

### Ingredients:

3 medium onions, finely chopped

6 cloves garlic, finely chopped

2 tbsp. olive oil

2 tbsp. butter

3 lb. stewing beef

4 tbsp. balsamic vinegar

2 14-oz. cans chopped tomatoes

3 tbsp. tomato puree

3 oz. dark bitter chocolate

$1\frac{1}{2}$ tsp. dried thyme

$\frac{1}{2}$ tsp. dried marjoram

salt and freshly ground black pepper

### *Directions:*

1.  Preheat oven to 325° F.

2.  Fry the onion and garlic gently in the oil and butter
    and transfer to a casserole dish when done.

3.  Meanwhile, cut the beef into $1\frac{1}{2}$ inch squares and fry
    until browned. Transfer to casserole dish.

4.  Add the vinegar to the pan and boil briefly, scraping
    the sediment from the bottom. Then add chopped
    tomatoes and tomato puree. Season well, add the
    chocolate broken into small pieces, the herbs, and
    about half a cup of water. Stir until the chocolate is
    melted, then transfer to the casserole dish.

5.  Add enough water to come just to the top of the
    meat. Bake for one and a half to two hours until the
    meat is tender, stirring once.

---

## Pineapple and Chocolate Cheesecake

*(12 small portions)*

### *Ingredients:*

3 oz. butter or margarine

1 packet plain chocolate wafer cookies (although
you probably only need about two-thirds of the
packet)

1 tin crushed pineapple

1 packet lemon Jello

2 oz. superfine granulated sugar

1 17-oz. carton of cream cheese

1 small tin pineapple rings (to decorate)

Dark glace cherries (to decorate)

About 2 oz. dark chocolate (to decorate)

### *Directions:*

1.  Put the butter in a large bowl and heat in the microwave only until melted.

2.  Put the chocolate wafer cookies on a tray and crush with a rolling pin. Add the crushed cookies to the melted butter and stir until thoroughly mixed.

3.  Press the cookie mixture into the base and sides of a 12 inch flan dish.

4.  Put the crushed pineapple into a sieve over a bowl to drain the excess liquid.

5.  Prepare the Jello mixture as instructed, adding 3 fluid ounces of the juice from the crushed pineapple.

6.  Into a large mixing bowl, put the cream cheese, the drained crushed pineapple, and the liquid Jello mixture. Stir thoroughly and add sugar to taste if needed. Put the cream cheese mixture into the

cookie and butter mixture and store in the fridge until set.

7. When set, decorate with half rings of pineapple and cherries round the edge and grated chocolate in the center.

# References
# and Resources

## Introduction

Dr. M. Scott Peck, a psychiatrist whose spiritual exploration has led him to become a Christian, is well worth reading. His titles include:

On personal growth and relationships:

*The Road Less Travelled* (Touchstone Books, 2003).

On journeying into faith:

*Further Along the Road Less Travelled* (Simon & Schuster, 1997).

On creating true community:

*A Different Drum* (Touchstone Books, 1998).

## Week Two

Antoine de Saint-Exupéry, *The Little Prince* (Harcourt Trade Publishers, 2000).

Graham Kendrick & Steve Thompson, "Teach Me to Dance" (Make Way Music, 1993).

## Week Three

Edward Bond, *Plays One* (Methuen, 1990).

## Postscript

Gerard W. Hughes, *Oh God, Why?* (Bible Reading Fellowship, 1993).

Also by Gerard W. Hughes:

On his own pilgrimages:
*In Search of a Way* (Doubleday Publishing, 1980).

On exploring your own spiritual journey:
*God of Surprises* (Cowley Publications, 1993).

## The Curious History of Chocolate

Information taken from:
Sophie D. and Michael D. Coe, *The True History of Chocolate* (Thames & Hudson, 2000).

## Ideas for a Chocolate Feast

### *Semi-sweet Chocolate Ganache*
adapted from:

Marcel Desaulniers, *Death by Chocolate—The Last Word on a Consuming Passion* (Virgin Books, 1992).

### Mole Poblano

adapted from:

Michael Barry, *Chocolate the Crafty Way* (Jarrold Publishing, 1998) and from *The True History of Chocolate*

### Beef with Balsamic Vinegar and Chocolate

adapted from:

Michael Barry, *Chocolate the Crafty Way* (Jarrold Publishing, 1998).

And, of course, most importantly:

*Chocolat,* Miramax 2000

Directed by Lasse Hallstrom

Cast: Juliette Binoche, Judi Dench, Alfred Molina, Lena Olin and Johnny Depp

Screenplay by Robert Nelson Jacobs

Based on the novel *Chocolat* by Joanne Harris (Penguin USA, 2000)